POWERBOAT
Instructor's Handbook

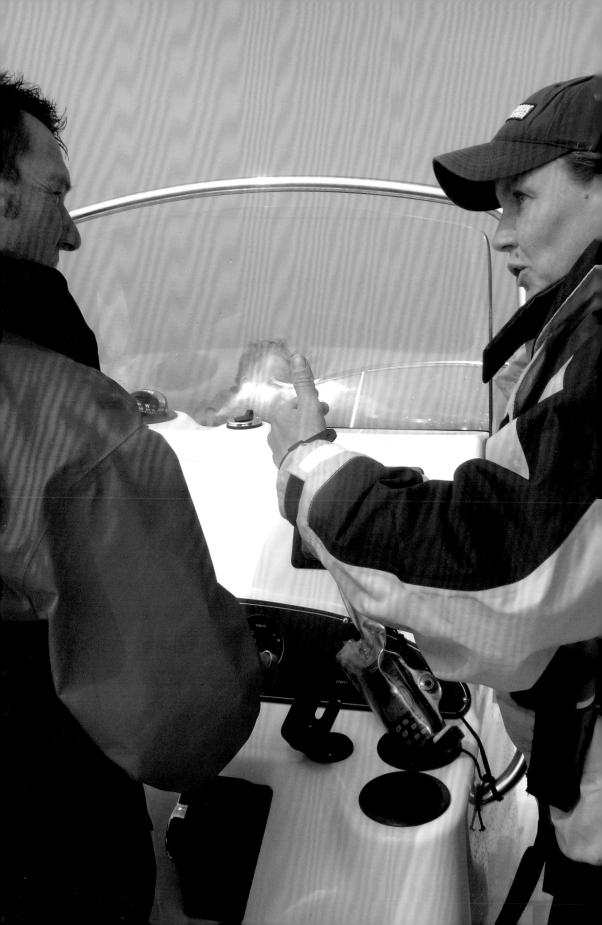

POWERBOAT
Instructor's Handbook

COLIN RIDLEY CLIVE GRANT
Edited by Paul Mara

RYA Introduction to Powerboat Instructors Handbook
Copyright RYA 2008

The Royal Yachting Association
RYA House
Ensign Way
Hamble
Southampton
SO31 4YA
Tel: 0845 345 0400
Fax: 0845 345 0329
E-mail: publications@rya.org.uk
Web: www.rya.org.uk

RYA Order Code **G19**

A CIP record of this book is available from the
British Library

Note: While all reasonable care has been taken in
the preparation of this book, the publisher takes
no responsibility for the use of the methods or
products or contracts described in the book.

Telephone 0845 345 0400 for a free copy
of our Publications Catalogue.

Design **Balley Design Limited**
Illustrator **Rob Brandt**

Printed in UK by **Sussex Litho Limited**

CONTENTS

FOREWORD

The RYA Powerboat Scheme is recognised as the most successful small boat training scheme in the world. It caters for novices and amateurs, through to professional operators wishing to use their RYA qualification commercially.

Paul Mara
RYA Chief Powerboat Instructor

This book is an invaluable companion for new and experienced instructors alike. It covers methods of instruction, learning styles, who can teach the scheme and where. Throughout the book you will find Top Tips on making your task as an instructor much easier and more enjoyable.

At the back of the book you will find a CD with useful teaching resources and short video clips to enhance your course presentation.

I hope that this book proves of value and that upon successful completion of your training I will be able to welcome you as an RYA Powerboat Instructor.

RYA CODE OF ETHICS AND CONDUCT FOR INSTRUCTORS, TRAINERS AND COACHES

SPORTS TRAINING AND COACHING HELPS THE DEVELOPMENT OF INDIVIDUALS THROUGH IMPROVING THEIR PERFORMANCE

This is achieved by:
- Identifying and meeting the needs of individuals
- Improving performance through a progressive programme of safe, guided practice, measured performance and/or competition
- Creating an environment in which individuals are motivated to maintain participation and improve performance

Instructors, trainers and coaches should comply with the principles of good ethical practice listed below. They must:
- If working with young people under the age of 18, have read and understood the Child Protection Policy as detailed on the RYA website at www.rya.org.uk under Working with Us
- Respect the rights, dignity and worth of every person and treat everyone equally within the context of their sport
- Place the well-being and safety of the student above the development of performance. Follow all guidelines laid down by the sport's governing body and hold appropriate insurance cover
- Develop an appropriate working relationship with students (especially children), based on mutual trust and respect and not exert undue influence to obtain personal benefit or reward
- Encourage and guide students to accept responsibility for their own behaviour and performance
- Hold relevant up to date and nationally recognised governing body qualifications
- Ensure that the activities they direct or advocate are appropriate for the age, maturity, experience and ability of the individual
- At the outset, clarify with students (and where appropriate their parents) exactly what is expected of them and what they are entitled to expect
- Always promote the positive aspects of their sport (eg. courtesy to other water users).
- Consistently display high standards of behaviour and appearance

01

RYA ORGANISATION

RYA TRAINING CENTRES
RYA TRAINING CENTRE RECOGNITION

RYA ORGANISATION

Courses within the RYA National Powerboat Scheme are organised by RYA Recognised Training Centres. These fall into three main groups:

- *Powerboating schools open to the public*
- *Sailing clubs which provide tuition to their members*
- *Restricted organisations such as Local Education Authorities, HM Forces, Lifeguards and other groups*

The principals of RYA Recognised Training Centres are the only persons authorised to issue RYA Powerboat Certificates.

RECOGNITION OF TRAINING CENTRES

Before recognition as a training centre can be granted, the proposed principal must complete an application form obtainable from the RYA and return it with a fee to cover the cost of initial inspection.

The centre will be visited, when fully operational, by an RYA Inspector and, subject to a satisfactory Inspector's Report, recognition will be granted by the RYA. Subsequent annual and "spot" inspections are carried out at the discretion of the RYA.

During the visit, the Inspector will ascertain that:

- *the principal or chief Instructor holds a valid RYA Powerboat Instructor certificate*
- *Instructor certificates are supported by a valid First Aid Certificate*
- *the centre's teaching syllabus meets the requirements of RYA certificate courses*
- *the onshore teaching facilities are adequate for the proposed operation*
- *the boats to be used for instruction are suitable, seaworthy and in good repair*
- *all students are in possession of personal buoyancy appropriate to the type of boat in which they are receiving instruction*
- *the principal properly understands the requirements of the RYA as to the proper running of an RYA Training Centre, particularly with regard to advertising and the nature of certificate and non-certificate courses*

The RYA will then classify the training centre on the basis of the Inspector's Report. Recognition for running the Safety Boat and Advanced courses will only be granted if a range of suitable boats and qualified instructors is available. This shall not prevent other centres being granted the authority to run practical assessments for Level 2 under Section D of the syllabus.

RYA recognition implies that some certificate courses are run and that the remainder are closely associated with the aims of the RYA National Powerboat Scheme.

Recognition of a training centre is vested in the principal and will automatically be revoked on a change of principal, discontinuance of active instruction or sale of the centre. A re-inspection must take place before recognition may be reinstated. Recognition may also be withdrawn if, in the opinion of the RYA, the standards of recognition are not being maintained.

An annual subscription is payable to the RYA, except in the case of recognised training centres which are already subscribing as clubs or associations. The annual recognition fee is waived for the year in which recognition is granted.

ADVERTISING AND USE OF RYA NAME

Only the principal of an RYA Recognised Training Centre may use the RYA's name in any advertising material e.g. signs, brochures and advertisements. Copies of the RYA logo suitable for printing are available to principals from the RYA Training Division.

Individual instructors and examiners may not use the RYA's name in any advertising or publicity material.

ADMINISTRATIVE PROCEDURES

On being granted recognition, each training centre may open an account with the RYA for bulk purchase of publications and certificates. The latter are supplied only to the principals of training centres.

The principal is responsible for ensuring that students' logbooks are correctly completed at the end of each course and that certificates are endorsed to show whether they have been gained on inland or coastal waters and in planing or displacement boats.

02

RYA POWERBOAT INSTRUCTOR

THE **RYA** POWERBOAT INSTRUCTOR

In this section of the book you will learn all about the role and how to become an RYA Powerboat Instructor

DEFINITION

The instructor is a competent and experienced powerboat handler who has been trained to teach powerboating up to the standard of the RYA National Powerboat Certificate, Level 2 under the supervision of the principal of an RYA Recognised Training Centre.

So you want to become a Powerboat Instructor...

BECOMING AN INSTRUCTOR

Candidates must fulfil the following criteria before taking part in the 3-day instructor training course:

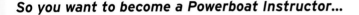

- *Minimum age 16. No candidates will be accepted for training under this age*
- *At least 5 seasons logged experience of powerboating, preferably in a range of boat types and sizes. For those who use powerboats as an integral part of their full time occupation this period is reduced to one season*
- *RYA National Powerboat Certificate Level 2*
- *Valid first aid certificate (either the RYA's First Aid Certificate, or one recognised by the Health and Safety Executive, covering the treatment of hypothermia and a minimum of six hours course length)*
- *Existing instructors wishing to teach the Safety Boat Course must hold that level of certificate themselves*
- *Existing instructors wishing to teach the Advanced course must hold that level of certificate themselves and attend a two-day endorsement course (Minimum age 17 years)*
- *Pass a Powerboat Instructor Skills Assessment before attending the three day instructor course*

An RYA Powerboat Instructor is not automatically qualified to teach courses – they may only do so at a suitably recognised RYA Training Centre.

A full list of RYA Training Centres offering RYA First Aid courses can be found on the RYA website (www.rya.org.uk).

Contact RYA HQ or your Regional Development Officer (RDO) or Regional Coach for a list of Instructor Courses. Information is also available on the Training section of the RYA website.

INSTRUCTOR TRAINING

Candidates should apply to their Regional Coach or RDO or the RYA Training Division for a list of local Instructor courses. (No candidate under the age of 16 will be accepted for Instructor training.) Candidates will attend an Instructor course run by an RYA Powerboat Trainer, including moderation by an independent trainer. The three day course includes:

• *Principles of practical instruction*

• *Lesson planning*

• *Teaching styles*

• *Use of questioning*

• *Preparation and use of visual aids*

• *Assessment of students' learning*

• *Explanation and presentation of theory subjects*

• *The structure of the National Scheme*

• *Planning progressive teaching sessions*

• *Preparation of boats and equipment*

• *Teaching methods to Level 2*

• *Assessment of the students' ability to instruct to an appropriate level using real students if possible*

POWERBOAT INSTRUCTOR SKILLS ASSESSMENT

Before attending the Instructor course potential instructor candidates must pass a Powerboat Instructor Skills Assessment with a Trainer. The assessment will be a test of your practical boat handling skills and depth of knowledge of the subject. You will be expected to demonstrate good skills to the standard of Powerboat level 2. Upon successful completion of the assessment, the Trainer will sign the candidates G20 Powerboat Logbook.

ASSESSMENT

Aim

To ensure that instructors reach a required minimum standard in personal ability, background knowledge and teaching ability.

Method

During the Instructor course, candidates will be assessed afloat and ashore, being judged on:

- *Technical ability and background knowledge*
- *Practical instruction afloat*
- *A shorebased training session*
- *Planning and organisation of small group tuition*
- *Communication skills, which will be continually assessed on and off the water.*

The intention of this method of assessment is to ensure that instructors can teach safely and competently.

TECHNICAL ABILITY/KNOWLEDGE

This will become clear during the course, both from the practical sessions and from candidates' input to shorebased discussions. Although background knowledge may not be tested formally, it will obviously affect candidates' responses to problems posed during the course.

PRACTICAL INSTRUCTION AFLOAT

Conventionally, three methods of assessment are possible:

- *With beginners, if the instructor course is run using guinea pig students*
- *Using other Instructor candidates as 'students'*
- *With the course trainer and moderator playing the part of the students*

The first method is preferred by many Powerboat trainers, as it provides the most realistic assessment. If the other methods are used, the Powerboat trainer will explain the roles played by him/herself and/or other instructors before each session. Candidates who are in any doubt about the briefing should ask for a further explanation.

The Powerboat trainers will be looking for:

- *Is the session safe, constructive an appropriate aim*
- *Good boat preparation*
- *A friendly, supportive manner towards students*
- *Good boat control at all times*
- *Teaching progression according to the students' ability*
- *Correct positioning of personnel in the boat*
- *Successful demonstrations and clear explanations*
- *Correct diagnosis and tactful correction of students' faults*

The candidate will be judged responsible for the boat and crew the whole time, even though they may not be at the controls. Conversely, the candidate who spends too long at the controls themselves, rather than reserving their driving for demonstrations, is unlikely to impress.

When beginners are used, the Powerboat trainer will also be assessing the candidate through their reaction, looking for the three key factors which are important for successful teaching:

- *Are the students safe?*
- *Are they learning anything valuable?*
- *Are they enjoying themselves?*

No weighting is put on any of these three, as they are inter-related. The good instructor meets each goal all the time.

ONSHORE TRAINING

Candidates are not expected to be professional lecturers or polished orators. In fact, the title of this part of the assessment has been deliberately chosen to allow a practical bias. The Powerboat trainer will be looking for:

- *Overall format clear - introduction, development and summary*
- *Audible, interesting voice - right speed of presentation*
- *Accurate, relevant content - sufficient material but not beyond what the syllabus demands*
- *Essential points emphasised and summarised*
- *Teaching aids prepared and used as appropriate*
- *Difficulties discovered and corrected*
- *Questions prompted and answered*
- *The most common fault of nervous, inexperienced candidates is to try to cram too much detail into the time available and then rush through it by speaking too quickly*

ORGANISING GROUP TUITION

During the course each candidate will be made responsible for one or more practical sessions, as outlined above. In assessing the organisation of these, the Examiner will be looking for:

Clear briefings
- *Was the aim clearly stated/agreed?*
- *Did the group know what was required?*
- *Were time/area limits defined?*
- *Was an "abandon session" signal agreed?*

Good group control afloat
- *Any unnecessary delays?*
- *Were problems identified and solved?*
- *Did the session achieve its aim?*
- *Did the group have fun and was a learning environment created?*

Clear debriefings

• *Were problems discussed – Ask – Discuss - Solve?*

• *Did instructors report progress?*

Good group control ashore

• *Was it obvious who was leading?*

• *Were the whole group involved?*

• *Was enthusiasm maintained?*

Good relationship with others

OVERALL ASSESSMENT

In addition to the detailed points outlined above, the Powerboat trainer will be making a subjective assessment of each candidate as an instructor, seeing how they match up to the instructor qualities detailed later in this book. In essence these can be summarised as –

• *Enthusiasm for the sport*
• *Confidence in the subject*
• *Teaching ability*
• *Awareness*
• *Anticipation*

Candidates should be given an indication of progress throughout the course and in a short debrief immediately after their practical sessions, but at the end of the course the Powerboat trainer will confirm whether or not each candidate has reached the required standard as an RYA Powerboat Instructor. The outcome should not come as a shock!

The Powerboat trainer will explain in detail to unsuccessful candidates the areas in which they have shortcomings, so that these may be overcome before future reassessment. This will be agreed between the trainer and the candidate and recorded in the G20 Powerboat logbook.

Upon successful completion of the course, candidates will have their G20 logbooks signed by the Powerboat trainer, who will forward a recommendation to the RYA for issue of the Powerboat Instructor Certificate.

COASTAL ENDORSEMENT

Candidates who are trained and assessed on coastal waters will have their Instructor certificates suitably endorsed. Those who are trained and assessed on inland waters will be required to attend a one-day coastal conversion course if they want to gain the Coastal Endorsement to their Instructor certificate.

PLANING/DISPLACEMENT

It is recognised that most Powerboat Instructor candidates will come from a planing boat background, however the RYA does not differentiate between planing and discplacement instructors. It is emcumbant upon the instructor to ensure that he teaches within his personal capabilities and does not instruct on a vessel that he is not fully familiar.

INSTRUCTOR COURSE OUTCOMES

Most candidates who meet the entry criteria and put in the required level of effort before and during their course will pass. In some cases, it may be that an individual is given an action plan - something that they need to do before being reassessed or appointed.

An action plan should not be seen as a negative outcome, indeed many candidates who pass will also receive an action plan related to their continuing development as a powerboat instructor.

Newly qualified instructors should expect to be asked to run their first course under the eye of another instructor, or assist on a course run by another instructor - a "safety net" that is often appreciated!

PROGRESSION

On passing an instructor course, it is recommended that new instructors run some Level 2 courses before progressing onto higher levels of tuition. If, when they pass their instructor course, they already hold the Safety Boat Certificate then they can teach to that level. If not, then attending, and passing, the Safety Boat Certificate will enable the instructor to teach to that level.

To teach the Intermediate and Advanced Courses the instructor must first complete the RYA Advanced Course and a 2 day RYA Advanced Instructor Endorsement Course. Gaining experience by working alongside, or simply observing, a qualified RYA Advanced Instructor is likely to provide a valuable insight to the standard required.

There is no requirement for the newly qualified RYA Level 2 Powerboat instructor to obtain further qualifications but they are likely to find that they become better instructors by doing so.

RYA POWERBOAT TRAINER

The RYA Powerboat trainer is an experienced RYA Advanced Powerboat instructor who has been trained and assessed as being suitable to train and assess others to all levels within the RYA Powerboat Scheme.

Powerboat trainer training is organised by the RYA which should be contacted for details of courses and to confirm their suitability. Alternatively, the appropriate RYA Regional Coach or Regional Development Officer will be able to provide details as the candidate will require a recommendation from their RDO or RC before being contacted by the RYA.

Those considering applying to become a Powerboat trainer should satisfy themselves that they understand EVERYTHING on all the RYA Powerboat Course syllabi – and can actually teach it. Observing an instructor course is a good way to ascertain strengths and development areas.

RYA NATIONAL POWERBOAT SCHEME

LEVEL	TITLE	DESCRIPTION
1	START POWERBOATING	A practical introduction to powerboating
2	NATIONAL POWERBOAT CERTIFICATE	Provides the skills and background knowledge needed by the competent powerboat driver and is the basis of the International Certificate of Competence
	INTERMEDIATE POWERBOAT CERTIFICATE	Covers practical use of pilotage and passage planning by day on coastal waters, using both traditional and electronic navigational techniques
	ADVANCED POWERBOAT CERTIFICATE	Provides the skills and background knowledge needed by powerboat drivers operating in coastal waters, in more demanding conditions
	SAFETY BOAT CERTIFICATE	Provides the skills required when acting as an escort craft, safety boat or coach boat for a fleet of dinghies, windsurfers or canoes, for racing or training activities

All activities must be supervised at all times by a person holding an appropriate and valid minimum RYA qualification:

ACTIVITY	SUPERVISED BY
POWERBOATING	Powerboat Instructor or Advanced Powerboat Instructor
PERSONAL WATERCRAFT	Personal Watercraft Instructor

No school may operate at an uninspected coastal site without an Advanced Powerboat Instructor

Student:Instructor ratios, as given in the appropriate RYA publications, should be observed for all courses, at all levels and at all times. For basic skills courses:

TYPE OF CRAFT	STUDENT:INSTRUCTOR RATIO
POWERBOATS	Levels 1 and 2 - 3:1, Safety Boat course - 6:1 (2 boats) Intermediate and Advanced course - 6:1 (2 boats)
PERSONAL WATERCRAFT	1 instructor can be responsible for up to 3 machines and 6 students. No more than 2 students per machine

For powerboat courses, up to 50% of helpers assisting an Instructor may be unqualified, but must be experienced and competent. As part of the centre's staff training programme, all assistants should be encouraged to gain RYA instructor qualifications.

RYA PERSONAL WATERCRAFT SCHEME

As part of recognition for personal watercraft you must have an RYA Personal Watercraft Instructor as the principal or Chief Instructor. Working under them should be other RYA Personal Watercraft Instructor(s) to meet the RYA student: instructor ratios.

Information is also available on the Training section of the website. www.ryatraining.org.uk

The Introduction to Personal Watercraft book (G35) is a useful reference book for you and your students.

Eligibility for the RYA Personal Watercraft Instructor course: Candidates must fulfil the following criteria before taking part in the 3-day Personal Watercraft Instructor training course:

- *Minimum age 16 years (no candidates will be accepted for training under this age)*
- *RYA Personal Watercraft Proficiency Certificate*
- *At least two year's experience of driving personal watercraft*
- *Valid first aid certificate (either the RYA's First Aid Certificate, or one recognised by the Health and Safety Executive, covering the treatment of hypothermia and of a minimum of 6 hours course length)*

Contact RYA HQ or your Regional Development Officer or Regional Coach for a list of Instructor Courses.

POWERBOAT/PERSONAL WATERCRAFT CHECKLIST

Ideally, both planing and displacement powerboats should be available. For Powerboating, the level of recognition will depend on the number and type of powerboats available, the availability of suitably qualified instructors, the type of water and the operating area of the centre.

Powerboats and Personal Watercraft operating at sea must be maintained and operated to the same standards as safety boats and powerboats must carry the equipment list specified for safety boats with the exception of the towing bridle.

Craft used for Level 2 and above tuition must have access to a GPS set, either fixed or hand held. Craft used for Intermediate and Advanced Courses must in addition have a depth sounder.

The Advanced and Intermediate Powerboat courses can only be run at coastal centres using planing boats. Centres are advised to use a "buddy system" as far as possible. The boat should be suitably equipped for short coastal passages and the following must be available: lights, compass, VHF radio, electronic navigation aid, torch, and flares. Also available ashore must be laminated charts, plotting instruments, tide tables and tidal stream information, and 150 Newton lifejacket fitted with DoT light on the Advanced course.

Kill-cords must be fully functional and must be fitted and used at all times.

Power boats with outboard engines must be fitted with effective kill-cords of the appropriate length. The lanyard is a cord usually between 4 and 5 feet (1220 and 1524mm) in length when stretched out. Craft used for 8-11 year old tuition must have 2 kill-cords. The purpose of the kill-cord is to prevent the driver from leaving the helm position either on purpose or by accident.

Outboard engines should be securely mounted. Fuel tank and battery fixings should be secure and adequate. Engines should have been serviced on a regular basis and be in good order. Boats should be seaworthy and in good condition at all times.

Centres running the Safety Boat Course should have a good variety of sailing and windsurfing craft readily available for use. It is unlikely that centres which are not attached to dinghy sailing and/or windsurfing clubs or larger dinghy sailing and windsurfing training centres will be recognised to train and assess candidates for RYA Safety Boat certificates.

The centre should ensure that trolleys/trailers are suitable for the craft and in a serviceable condition. The trolleys should enable the craft to be safely launched, recovered and manoeuvred on land without risk of injury to the users.

OWN BOAT TUITION

In addition to offering courses using the Centre's own boats, some centres also offer tuition in a student's own boat. Powerboat Instructors can conduct tuition on a student's own boat provided that it is from the RTCs normal operating site. Advanced Instructors can carry out own boat tuition away from the RTCs normal site. The boat should be equipped to a similar standard to that of a centres boat. It should be noted that the owner is the skipper and is responsible for insuring the craft. All conditions of recognition concerning shore-based facilities, course length, safety equipment, etc, apply. A centre may not, however, offer only own boat tuition.

INSTRUCTOR QUALIFICATION	QUALIFIED TO TEACH
POWERBOAT INSTRUCTOR (INLAND)	Levels 1 and 2 (Inland)
POWERBOAT INSTRUCTOR WITH SAFETY BOAT ENDORSEMENT (INLAND)	Levels 1 and 2 plus Safety Boat (All Inland)
POWERBOAT INSTRUCTOR WITH COASTAL ENDORSEMENT	Levels 1 and 2 (Inland and Coastal)
POWERBOAT INSTRUCTOR WITH SAFETY BOAT AND COASTAL ENDORSEMENT	Levels 1 and 2 plus Safety Boat (Inland and Coastal)
ADVANCED POWERBOAT INSTRUCTOR	Levels 1 and 2 (Inland and Coastal) Intermediate & Advanced (Coastal only)
ADVANCED POWERBOAT INSTRUCTOR WITH SAFETY BOAT	Levels 1 and 2, Safety Boat (Inland and Coastal) Intermediate & Advanced (Coastal only)
POWERBOAT TRAINER	Levels 1 and 2, Safety Boat (Inland and Coastal) Intermediate, Advanced & Instructor Training Courses
PERSONAL WATERCRAFT INSTRUCTOR	Personal Watercraft Proficiency Course
PERSONAL WATERCRAFT TRAINER	Personal Watercraft Instructor Training Course

*RYA Powerboat and Personal Watercraft courses may only be run at an RYA Training Centre. For details of how to become recognised, please contact the RYA Training department for an information pack or visit the **RYA website: www.ryatraining.org***

03

METHODS OF INSTRUCTION

METHODS OF INSTRUCTION

This section introduces the important qualities that an instructor should have and develops these qualities through considering student learning styles, presentation techniques and visual aid selection.

INSTRUCTOR QUALITIES

It would be very easy to make a list of important instructor qualities and expect all instructors to demonstrate each of these in the desired proportions. However, each instructor is an individual and their own flair, enthusiasm and interest in powerboating are key to the way they deliver their courses. So with this individualism as the starting point, what makes a good instructor?

At school most people had a favourite teacher. Imagine that person for a moment. What qualities did they demonstrate that made them your favourite? Why did you want to go to their lessons?

Assuming your response to education was positive, the qualities you have identified can be considered as qualities that you too should try to emulate.

The following list details some of the qualities that are often suggested:

Professional	Confident	Humour	Caring
Team Player	Consistent	Organised	Open
Interesting	Disciplined	Considerate	Subtle
Experienced	Simplifies things	Knowledgeable	Honest
Planner	Motivator	Responsible	Fair
Prepared	Balanced	Helpful	Punctual
Human	Good Control	Natural	Fun
Interested	Understanding	Respectful	Gives praise
Communicator	Enthusiastic	Competent	Keen
Patient	Amusing	Good explanations	Coach
Teacher	Sensitive	Tactful	Trusting
Good Delivery	Straight forward	Resourceful	Flexible
Approachable	Safety conscious	Conscientious	Supportive

There is no significance to the order shown, nor is the list exhaustive; there are no RYA required proportions an instructor has to demonstrate, and few if any of these qualities can be changed during an instructor course. Nevertheless an awareness that you could work to develop your skills in one of these qualities is an important lesson for any instructor to learn. One of the most important skills any candidate learns on an instructor course is the ability to develop their own instructor qualities.

WHAT MAKES A GOOD INSTRUCTOR?

Some instructors always seem to be natural and confident. More than likely that have had to practice to achieve this and have a well prepared session.

Communication is a two way process - be prepared to send and receive

   Confidence is probably the first thing people normally notice about an instructor, or more importantly, their lack of it. Two things help confidence:

Knowledge

a) Do I know enough to present this topic without talking rubbish?

b) Can I answer the most likely questions?

c) Do I have a plan for this topic?

If you cannot answer yes to these questions then you need to do some preparation before starting the presentation.

Usage

Confidence will increase with practice. The more you present, the more your confidence will grow. Few instructors completely get rid of nerves and even the most experienced instructors will be nervous at times. However, the good instructor has the ability to keep any lack of confidence from his/her students. Your students need a confident instructor so that they can have confidence in him/her too.

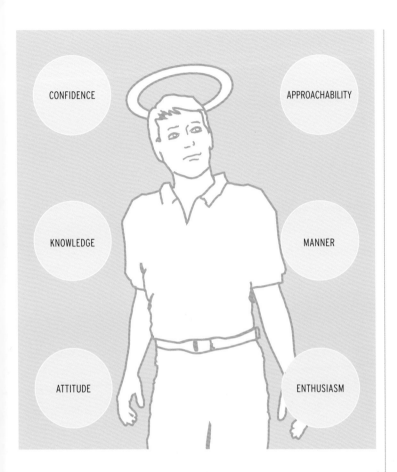

COMMUNICATION SKILLS

As an instructor you will always be told that good communication skills are vital for success. But what exactly are communication skills and what makes them good or bad? This section looks at this topic and gives ideas to ensure that the right message is sent to the student.

What exactly are communications?

Communication could be described as "an interaction with someone". In fact, the dictionary definition of "communicate" is "to impart, to give a share of, to transmit, to reveal". Notice that the definition does not mention anything about the way this is done. Specifically, it does not differentiate between verbal and non-verbal communication. Within this concept you must also appreciate that the message being sent may or may not be wanted; may or may not be expected, and may or may not be appreciated by the recipient, or recipients. Communication skills must include this understanding.

So, for our purposes we will define communications as "anything done, written, said or implied by one person that is understood or indeed misunderstood by another".

Don't forget that communication is a two way process and a message will be sent with the intention that someone else will be receiving it. Communication is about the two way process, not just about the transmitting part. And it's often more a case of not "what is said", but rather "what is not."

The definition given earlier included the possibility that a message may be misunderstood. Good communication skills are all about removing this risk so that the message gets to it's destination as intended. For the instructor this is vital.

SENSE AND LEARNING

We all learn through the use of a variety of inputs. When we think of instructing we often only consider the spoken word. However, sight is much more important in terms of understanding. In this section we consider the main inputs for learning.

"Positive body language, (what you don't say), will add to the value of what you do say"

We noted earlier that communications do not have to be verbal. Referring to the learning modes statistics:

Sight accounts for around 75%, hearing for around 13%, touch for 6%, taste for 3% and smell for 3%.

With such a significant component of the learning experience being related to sight you will see why we should make our course delivery as visual as possible. Why simply describe an object where it would be possible to show it?

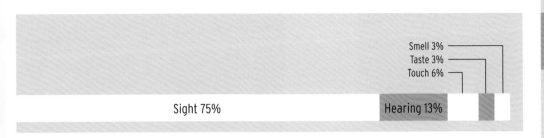

Smell 3%
Taste 3%
Touch 6%

Sight 75%

Hearing 13%

These statistics raise an important question, - How were they measured? Whilst it could appear that these values are questionable, and there are other sets of figures from different sources which differ slightly, most agree that the sense of sight is, by far, the most powerful of the human inputs.

Sensory Impairment

If an individual does not have the benefit of sight, it does not automatically follow that their information input (or learning capability) is deficient by 75%! On the contrary, the unaffected senses are likely to have become much more highly developed, e.g. the visually impaired tend to develop very acute senses of hearing, touch and smell, more so than the fully sighted. This ability of the various senses to compensate for defects in another means that there should be no reduction in the learning potential of individuals. There may merely be a change in the method of information gathering, which in turn dictates that a different style of delivery will help them to achieve.

Note that where impairment affects how the student is able to undertake a task, the "endorsements" section of the powerboat certificate allows for a comment such as "the holder should be accompanied by an able-bodied crew" or something similar.

BODY LANGUAGE & NON-VERBAL COMMUNICATIONS

Body language can be very revealing but it is not always an exact science, particularly in a multi-cultural situation. So, whilst it is worth considering what positive and negative body language you or your students exhibit, you have to be careful about how you interpret it.

Positive Language

Positive body language is usually less liable to misinterpretation! For instance, a relaxed posture suggests open for communication. Too much may give a "couldn't care less" attitude!

Good eye contact indicates interest in that person. It probably best to look away from time to time so as not to appear to be staring at the other person and ditch the sunglasses!

In most parts of the world, nodding indicates agreement and understanding. However continually bobbing your head up and down can be distracting!

Taking notes shows interest and involvement. This is especially so if the notes are relevant to the topic being covered.

Leaning closer and reducing the distance between two people indicates that interest is up and barriers are down.

Negative Language

Negative body language is often less reliable as an indicator of the person's comfort with the current situation. It may be that the other person is simply more comfortable that way. For instance, arms folded in front may suggest a barrier or resistance to what is being said or the person may simply be more comfortable that way.

A hand over one's mouth is a closed gesture. Leaning on one's elbow with the chin in the hand can communicate boredom. Arms behind the head, leaning back – between friends this can be a relaxed gesture. In a student/instructor situation it can indicate a desire to demonstrate who is in charge.

"It's that "added thing" which is so hard to quantify which makes the use of positive body language so important"

Verbal versus Non-verbal communication

Hearing accounts for just 13% of a person's sensory input. Try watching a football match on TV with the volume turned down and you will appreciate how little you actually miss! However, what is not said accounts for 87% of an individuals' sensory input. Try going to a football match and by simply listening without any commentary see how difficult it is to work out what's going on.

It's the visual component which when missing causes us problems - and hence why this is such an important topic.

Facial expressions

The expressions below showing only the eyes and eyebrows, will each give you an idea of someone in a different mood. You should be able to spot surprise, anxiety, boredom and concern fairly easily.

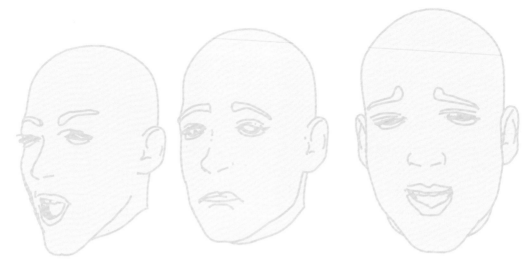

Of course, there is much more to it than that and the cartoon caricatures shown above each send different messages.

For an Instructor

Just as the non-verbal image the instructor displays will affect the students, the instructor should also be in "receive mode" so that he or she can read messages sent back from the students. If the students are yawning there is a good chance that the presentation is boring. Alternatively, if they are looking interested then they may actually be interested!

This instant feedback is vital for the instructor and allows the presentation technique to be changed if appropriate.

BRIEFING AND DEBRIEFING

Students always want to know what they are about to do, and why. How does this activity lead towards the objectives of their course? This is the briefing.

At the end of the activity the students will also want to know how they have done. Specifically, how has their progress matched up to the required standard? This is the debriefing and is a two way communication process.

Giving feedback in a debrief

Feedback is an important component of the learning process but it needs to be structured if it is to be of any use to the student. Unstructured feedback will, at best, be useless. At worst, it will cause the student to feel challenged and they will doubtless react accordingly.

Practicing a skill is not enough to learn it correctly. It needs to be accompanied by feedback to help improvement or to reassure the students, (or instructor), that they are on course. Feedback can come from either the students or the instructor and this makes it an indispensable part of the learning process - the student cannot get the feedback from anyone else.

At its simplest form feedback could be a simple "well done" or a nod of approval. However, if this is overdone then it soon loses any value. Feedback could also be a chat about how you have just performed ... or it could be a formal meeting - set at a time and place so as to avoid unwanted interruptions.

Feedback is the aspect of the instructor's role that is one of the more difficult, yet satisfying. The whole purpose of the instructor being there is to help correct faults and so see an improvement in the student's performance.

The student's feedback does not only come from the instructor, but also from their own learning process, but this creates a problem. All too frequently the student gets it wrong and thinks it went well when it didn't or thinks it was a disaster when it was actually quite good.

So, leave them time to assimilate their own thoughts but don't leave it too long and certainly don't leave them doing things wrong before you suggest an alternative approach. Remember, usually the student knows that something has gone wrong. They don't need feedback to realise that they have just hit a buoy, and the time to discuss what went wrong is not whilst they are trying to stop the air escaping from a hole in the sponson! At the right moment, all that may be needed is some input to make the next attempt work better! However, don't jump on mistakes as students can, and will, learn if they are able to learn from their own mistakes.

The location and nature of the activity are certain to affect the timing and frequency of feedback. It is impractical to stop an activity whilst in full flow unless it is so wrong that to continue could be unsafe. In the same way, the location and formality needed may reflect the importance of the feedback and show for instance that you consider this serious or, maybe, that you have set aside some special time for this person.

Be positive in what you say when giving feedback. Negative feedback will not encourage learning whereas positive feedback

encourages the students to have a go, even if it ultimately goes wrong. Good feedback will act as a stimulus to the students.

There are two types of feedback. The first and most likely will be informal feedback, given during an activity.

The second will be more formal, where some time has been set aside for an individual student and an instructor to consider progress and suggest an action plan, if appropriate. During an instructor course you are likely to offer some formal feedback by way of a mid-course debrief.

For informal feedback, try to draw from the student what they thought was wrong and so help them solve the problem. Provide no more information than is necessary and try to help them work it out rather than simply telling them the answer. One way of starting this process is to ask the student to reflect back on what they actually did.

To be helpful, feedback to an individual must be such that the person receiving it:
• *understands the feedback*
• *is able to accept the feedback*
• *is able to do something about it*

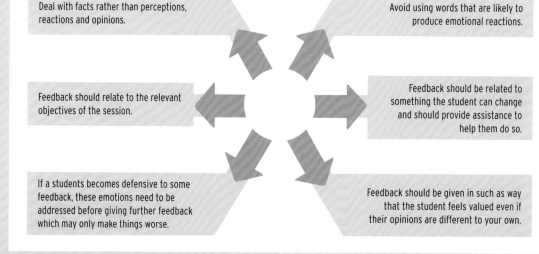

Deal with facts rather than perceptions, reactions and opinions.

Avoid using words that are likely to produce emotional reactions.

Feedback should relate to the relevant objectives of the session.

Feedback should be related to something the student can change and should provide assistance to help them do so.

If a students becomes defensive to some feedback, these emotions need to be addressed before giving further feedback which may only make things worse.

Feedback should be given in such as way that the student feels valued even if their opinions are different to your own.

The subject of feedback could and, indeed, does fill entire books. However, there are six major "must do's" which can help to make feedback constructive:

A common approach to giving good feedback is to follow the "feedback model". This essentially has three stages and is sometimes referred to as the "hamburger".

1. *Build the students' confidence with things they did right. Although they have just hit the pontoon quite hard they must have done something right - even if it was only remembering the way to approach the pontoon allowing for wind and tide!*

2. *Now return to reality by considering what was not so good and suggest ways to put it right. Don't start this with "but", use "however".*

3. *Finally suggest/agree an action plan.*

A typical conversation using the "feedback model" might go as follows:

"Jo, I was particularly pleased to see that you remembered … and… However, what happened when you approached the pontoon…….
How could you have changed that…? What would you do differently the next time…? Then the conversation starts with both the trainer and the student identifying points and offering solutions. In this way the development areas are identified by both the trainer and the student. The last phase is to consolidate the learning and to find a positive point ."

Remember, you want students to repeat the good parts and develop the problem areas.

It is always easier to tell someone that they have just done well, or they have passed. Very seldom do they ask why, nor does the instructor tell them. Tell them that their performance was not up to standard and the question "why?" will be one of the first you hear, unless you have addressed this in your feedback. One method is to ask them to reflect back on what they have just done, make them focus in on what they have actually achieved, what went well and where the development areas were. If they enter into a conversation they will feel more at ease and talk openly in a non judgemental conversation.

For this reason, it is not uncommon for a student to be told they have passed whereas they (with their instructor's help) really needed to improve their performance. Remember that powerboating courses are not attendance awards!

The "F" (fail) word is never used and there is no suggestion of failure. What has been suggested is that the student may need a little more time/practice. Properly managed, your students will thank you for an honest debrief that tells them they have not yet passed, or are not yet competent.

Of course, giving feedback like this is much easier if the instructor discussed possible course outcomes at the start of the course.

RECEIVING FEEDBACK

Feedback for the instructor is just as important and can come from several directions - although, hopefully, not at the same time and, hopefully, not contradictory.

Firstly, the instructor can expect feedback from his chief instructor - be it a more senior Powerboat instructor they are working with or the principal. They will have been watching the instructor ashore and afloat, with students and whilst working as part of the instructor team.

Secondly, the instructor can expect feedback from their students. The form this takes may vary from a simple "thank-you" at the end of a session to something specific mentioned in the end of course evaluation form.

Thirdly, is feedback from someone who has been watching the activity but who is not directly connected with it – maybe a teacher watching you with their students.

It is important to remember that feedback from some groups

of students may be rather more direct than you might have anticipated. Children are not usually inhibited in giving instant feedback and are likely to tell you bluntly the way it is. Adults, on the other hand will tend to be more guarded and simply imply on the course evaluation form that the instructor's background knowledge was "satisfactory" rather than "good".

Regardless of the source, there are certain skills to receiving feedback.

Feedback received is always about something that did or did not happen - not current or future events. In this way, receiving feedback always offers the possibility of learning something which can be used as the basis for further improvement.

Just as there are some steps to consider for giving feedback, so too there are steps for receiving it:

1. Listen carefully.

2. Try not to be defensive if you feel it is wrong, but mentally note questions or disagreements.

3. Paraphrase what you think you have heard to check your perception.

4. Ask questions to clarify and ask for examples in those areas which are unclear or you disagree with.

5. Carefully assess the accuracy and value of what you have heard.

6. If necessary, gather further information from other sources or by watching your own behaviour and other peoples' reactions to it.

7. Do not overreact to feedback, but, where necessary, modify your actions accordingly and then assess how this changes what you do. Remember the "Behaviour – Attitude cycle" . Your behaviour will affect their attitude which will affect your attitude which will affect their behaviour, someone has to break the cycle in a negative cycle.

THE FEEDBACK FORM

Remember the saying "If you enjoyed your course tell a friend, if you didn't then tell us"? Well, that's a starter for considering the evaluation form. However, getting useful feedback from students is about a bit more than that.

At the end of a course, it is usual to be given an evaluation form. However, only do this if you are prepared to find that everything is not as good as you expected and that you are prepared to act on the feedback. Without these prerequisites, the feedback form is of limited use. This means reading the forms. If you don't want to use feedback forms consider how you are going to monitor standards... asking students if they enjoyed their course is generally not an effective method. If it was not very good they are unlikely to say so directly!

By all means include tick boxes for students to indicate their level of satisfaction with particular things such as the "quality of onshore teaching facilities" and the "suitability of the sailing area for the course". But, accept that the answers will only show you the level of satisfaction - not the reason why.

The best questions are those which demand a written response - but be careful not to ask too many or the boxes will be left unanswered, or in the worst cases the form will be ignored altogether.

To demonstrate that you are concerned with quality, you could ask questions such as:

- "If we could do one thing to improve the course what would that be?"
- "What will you tell your friends about your course"

Acting on the feedback is essential if you are to maintain standards and try to improve them. So, if a student suggests that they would have liked more time to practice a particular manoeuvre ... do you change your plan immediately? Maybe not. However, it would be wise to reflect on the session and consider:

- *Did you rush it?*
- *Did you explain it well enough?*
- *Was your demonstration of the exercise clear enough?*
- *Was that student was not given a fair go at the exercise?*
- *Was that student one of the minority who may find 2 days for a Level 2 course a bit challenging?*

Level 1 Powerboat courses are designed for a wide range of ages from 8 years old upwards. Do you give an 8 year old an evaluation form? Most centres probably do not. However, this discerning age group will want to come back if their course was enjoyable so their opinion is very valuable indeed. The problem with gathering feedback from the younger age group is that their written methods of expression may not work with your standard evaluation forms. Get creative - you need their input! 8 years olds grow up and are likely to return if their experience was favourable.

Since the feedback form is the student's way of assessing you, it makes sense for them to know the assessment criteria at the start of their course. Why not have a copy of the feedback form displayed on the wall so that they see at the outset the questions they will be asked to consider.

LEARNING STYLES

People learn in different ways and if your instruction is appropriately directed the student is likely to learn faster and have a more positively memorable experience. Experts in this field, Peter Honey and Alan Mumford, determined that there are four main learning styles. These are; Activist, Reflector, Theorist and Pragmatist.

ACTIVIST

Activists like to be involved in new experiences. They learn more when, for instance, they are thrown in the deep end with a difficult task. They tend to learn less when they are listening to lectures or long explanations.

Reflectors like to stand back and look at a situation from different perspectives. They tend to learn more when they have the opportunity to review what has happened and think about what they have learned. Unlike Activists, Reflectors tend to learn less when they are thrown in the deep end with a difficult task.

REFLECTOR

Theorists adapt and integrate observations into complex and logically sound theories. They think problems through in a step by step way. They tend to be perfectionists who like to fit things into a rational scheme. Theorists learn best when they are in structured situations with clear purpose and they learn less when the activity is unstructured or briefing is poor.

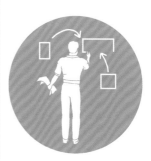

THEORIST

Pragmatists are keen to try things out. They tend to be impatient with lengthy discussions and are practical and down to earth. They learn best when they have the chance to try out techniques with feedback. They learn less when there is no practice or guidelines on how to do it.

PRAGMATIST

So, how can this knowledge be useful to an instructor? You cannot give every student a learning styles questionnaire at the beginning of the course. Rather, you might be able to agree with them how they would like you to deliver the course.

INFORMATION/FEEDBACK   PROCESSING/LEARNING STYLE

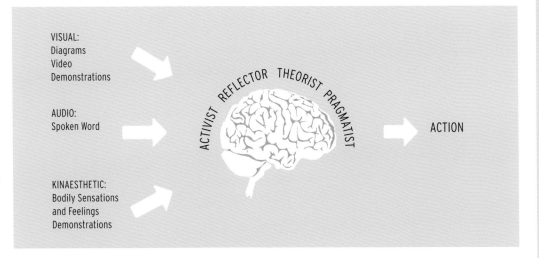

VISUAL:
Diagrams
Video
Demonstrations

AUDIO:
Spoken Word

KINAESTHETIC:
Bodily Sensations
and Feelings
Demonstrations

ACTIVIST REFLECTOR THEORIST PRAGMATIST

ACTION

PRESENTATION TECHNIQUES

Presentations

So, what exactly is a "presentation"? It could be almost anything from a lecture at an RYA conference, to a discussion with your Centre principal about a new idea you have. It could also be delivering a topic from a Level 2 course to one or more students. So, a presentation may have one or more of the following aims:

• *To teach or improve performance*
• *To persuade a group or people to do something*
• *To help students understand a topic better*

Some instructors always seem to give good presentations but are their skills natural or have they put some time and effort into improving their presentation skills? A good presentation will need some preparation - who are the intended students? What is their

A full online version of the Honey & Mumford Learning Styles Questionnaire is available from www.peterhoney.com on a pay-as-you-go basis for £10. The results include a full report with suggestions about how to become a more effective learner.

starting knowledge? What is your message to them? What options are there for the location to deliver the presentation?

This section is not intended to be definitive but rather to act as a reminder to those who consider themselves to be a polished presenter, and as a source of ideas to those who are less experienced.

The Presenter

The instructor has a particular responsibility not only to achieve their own objectives but also to help the students achieve theirs. The content of the presentation will be discussed later but for now we'll just consider first impressions.

Making the Right First Impression

What impression are you likely to gain from an instructor who arrives late, is unprepared and looks untidy? Whatever the impression it is likely to leave the instructor with an uphill struggle to convince you that they do know what they are talking about after all.

First impressions are very important and a professional delivery will have your students attention from the outset. Give your students the wrong first impression of you and you already have an upward slope to convince them that they were wrong. Thinking of it another way, all your students are doing is sizing you up - just like you size other people up. Subsequently, the reactions you get from your students will use this first impression or assumptions as the starting point.

First impressions are particularly important for presenting or lecturing to a younger audience who may think of the instructor as a role model. Make sure that it's the sort of model you want them to copy.

So what gives a good or bad impression?

When your students arrive there are a number of things that can happen. They can hang around in a foyer waiting for you to arrive. You can be late. You may not be expecting them, or you may have the wrong names!

Or ...

You could be there in good time to welcome the students into your classroom with a smile, your name and the course title being written on the board, with a register or attendance list to tick off who has arrived. While you wait for the rest to arrive you could show an interest in your students, asking, for example, how far they have travelled and offering a tea or coffee.

In effect, the initial contact and interest has also enabled you to find out a bit about your students and, with the right type of questions, you can identify their reason for doing the course so that your delivery can be made more personal. Looking back to learning styles - your first contact with the student will provide some insight.

The fact that you have shown an interest should make a good first impression. **So ...**

DO... Set a good example particularly with respect to dress, attitude to authority, responsibility and personal habits (e.g. time keeping, not smoking)

DO NOT... Be critical of others, make political statements, be racist or sexist etc.

THE LEARNING EXPERIENCE

Having seen what a good presentation is all about, we need to know a little more about the learning process. Consider the instructor and your students as two way radios. What can go wrong?

One or other might not be switched on – they are not listening. When passing on a message make sure that you have your students' attention. Watch your students and listen to their questions. This will help you decide whether your message is getting across. If it isn't, then adjust your style accordingly but don't change your style if it is working!

The radios are tuned to different frequencies – in this case your students fail to receive the message being sent out. The fault may have occurred at either end. However, it is the job of the instructor to spot this and to find another way of putting his message across.

The sound is distorted – the message received by your students is technically incorrect. Know your subject and make sure that everything you say is correct and not open to interpretation.

The channel keeps changing - changing your style or approach midway through your presentation will lose your students' attention fairly quickly.

One radio switches off half way through - your students have become bored, or more likely, you have become boring. Keep the content lively and interesting. Maintain your enthusiasm.

Your students think they have tuned into a foreign channel - avoid using unnecessary jargon and buzz-words. New terminology your students need to know may require further explanation for them to fully understand.

Authority

The instructor is likely to start with an element of credibility simply by being the instructor. However you need to maintain credibility and may be able to achieve this in a number of ways:

- *being knowledgeable about what you are talking about and honest about the knowledge you have*
- *if you make a point make it about something worthwhile*
- *be enthusiastic and sincere in what you say and aware of how you say it*
- *don't hide behind your qualifications*
- *avoid sarcasm or rudeness*

But why and how do people learn?

HOW DO PEOPLE LEARN?

The Learning Cycle

Learning involves developing knowledge from a known point into the unknown. Subsequently, that new knowledge is further developed into the unknown. In this way the learning cycle is just that, a cycle.

"Your students need to be warm enough to be comfortable and cool enough to stay awake"

The cycle involves establishing a safe learning environment where it is OK to make a mistake and where the supportive instructor helps to promote progress. Before an activity is undertaken the student needs to be given a briefing. He needs to know why the topic is relevant. Within the activity, the instructor demonstrates what is required; the students have a go (with input); then they show that they can do the task unassisted. Finally, the debrief lets them know how they have performed and provides areas that they may need to work on.

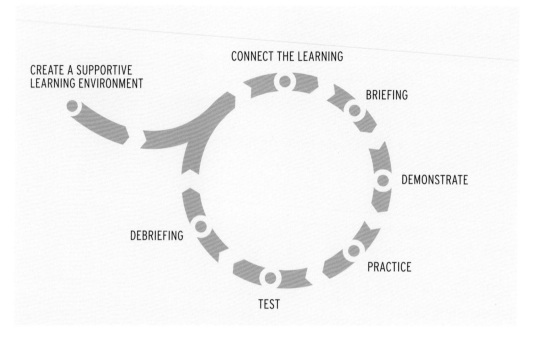

CREATE A SUPPORTIVE LEARNING ENVIRONMENT

CONNECT THE LEARNING

BRIEFING

DEMONSTRATE

PRACTICE

TEST

DEBRIEFING

Concentration

Nobody can learn without concentration and the instructor must keep an eye on the concentration level of their students. Instructors may need to vary the activity during the presentation or break up a long presentation by taking questions, using demonstrations to reinforce a point, or by practical examples.

WHY DO PEOPLE LEARN?

Understand why your students want to learn and you can work out the best way to teach them. The best instructors can deliver the same topic in a variety of ways - and may need to do so if they are teaching adults on one course and teenagers on another.

Beyond this obvious difference, the course introduction session should have enabled you to know why your students were on your course. Maybe they are thinking of getting a boat, maybe they need the qualification for their employment, maybe they are simply interested in powerboating? There must be a reason for learning and the instructor needs to know. The most common reasons might be: **interest, enthusiasm, competition, importance and relevance, stimulus.**

Barriers to Learning

We have already considered why people learn. The instructor also needs to know why their students might not. The barriers to learning are too numerous to cover in detail here. However, there are some common areas mainly concerned with the environment.

Temperature - *Your students need to be warm enough to be comfortable and cool enough to stay awake. Unfortunately, the ideal conditions may be different for each member of your group! This may be difficult to notice and there's every chance that if you get too engrossed in the presentation you may only notice the problem when you see your students yawning.*

Space - *Not too big and not too small.*

Distractions - *Noise or people walking past an open door/window are likely to be distracting to both students and instructor*

Light and air - *Make sure the room is lit properly, but not so bright that your students cannot see the image from the projector if you are using one,.*

Lack of incentive - *This is the biggest barrier of all. Your students need an incentive to listen or learn. Your introduction should provide them with the answer to "what am I going to get out of this?" Devise your objective clearly.*

Level - *Pitch the level of your presentation at the level of your students. Young people need to be taught or lectured to using a different approach to adults. Beginners in a subject need to be instructed using a different approach to the more experienced. Know your students and adapt your presentation to their needs.*

Ability *- Some of your students will pick up what you say more quickly than others. You may actually need two or more presentation for different ability groups.*

TYPES OF PRESENTATIONS

The size of your group will have a great effect on the best method of delivering your message. So too will your preferred style of delivery. Remember, though, that your group will usually consist of no more than six students. A lecture is probably not going to be appropriate. So what other types of "presentation" are there?

A "workshop" or "discussion" is often the best way to work with smaller groups. It is highly interactive, with the instructor guiding the students through an agenda. The instructor provides input as needed, and through questions and answers ensures that the students have the required knowledge of the subject. However, if this is not a natural way for the instructor to work it may appear that the instructor does not know the answer and is trying to see if the students can help him/her out. Done well it is a very slick way of working with the presentation, progressing at the students' pace.

A lecture may be appropriate in a small number of cases. Generally, this will be where no input is required or wanted through the presentation and questions are only taken at the end.

Briefing sessions are presentations too and require just as much thought. What is to be included, and how can this best be put across, needs consideration to be given to the location - often outside and just before an activity is to take place. Be careful that the briefing does not become a lecture - it's only intended to be brief!

A practical session is our most likely presentation. 90% of a Powerboat Level 2 course can probably be done in a practical environment. Even chartwork can be done on the boat allowing students to actually see the things that the symbols are portraying.

Whatever the type of session delivery you decide upon, try to make the session interactive. Ask questions, and listen to the answers. This enables you to check for an understanding of the topic and helps control the pace of your delivery. Once you have established that it's OK for your students to ask a question when they are unsure what you mean – you will find their progress becomes much quicker.

PRESENTATION PLANNING

However good the instructor his visual aids, his efforts will be wasted if he has not planned what he is going to say. You do not really need a script but you need a minimum of a "route-map" to help you remember what you want to cover next.

Deciding what to talk about, or rather, how much of what you know should be included, is probably the most difficult part of planning. To help you in this process start by trying to consider "learning objectives". Specifically, why should your students want to listen to you - what are their objectives?

Objectives are quite simply what you want your students to get out of the presentation - so it's a good place to start for planning what to cover. A good idea is to also refer to the appropriate course syllabus in the G20 Powerboating Logbook to make sure that your objectives are appropriate. Objectives are usually written by completing the following sentence - "By the end of this presentation students should be able to " - followed by the appropriate actions and performance verb. For example - "By the end of this presentation students should be able to list the three rules for setting good objectives".

Three rules for good objectives

1. The first rule is to use very specific verbs, such as list, identify, compare, etc. The best verbs are those that involve some action on the part of the student - they should have to do something - which results in better retention. Avoid verbs such as "know", "learn", "understand" as they are too vague and difficult to measure.

2. The second rule is that the objectives should have a measurable standard. In other words, you should be able to evaluate whether your presentation has been successful. To this end it is important that the objectives are shared with the students at the beginning of the presentation.

If you have good objectives, measurement is easy. Note the example used above - "Students should be able to list the three rules for setting good objectives". That is very specific and straight forward to assess by simply asking questions at the end of the presentation. **Consider the difference in style of presentation by these two alternatives...**

a. *"By the end of this presentation students should understand how to put on a lifejacket".*

b. *"By the end of this presentation students should be able to demonstrate how to put on a lifejacket".*

The second objective is certain to encourage a more active presentation, with a defined, measurable achievement level.

3. *The third rule is that the objectives should be reasonable. In other words, do the conditions exist that will allow you to achieve the objectives in the time and with the resources you have available?*

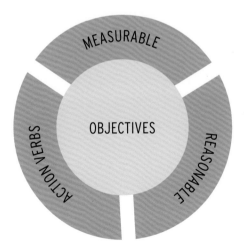

The objectives you now have define the scope of your presentation. Knowing this, your students, the time available and the location for the presentation, their prior knowledge and possibly their learning style, you can now proceed to develop your "route-map", using a "three step plan".

The Three Step Plan

1. *Write all that you know about the subject onto a large sheet of paper in the form of headings. If you can, try to group related things together. Even subjects which may not initially seem relevant to the presentation may help identify other things which are.*

2. *Keeping your objectives in mind, sort out the relevant material using the "MoSCow" technique - Must know, Should know, Could know. Keep in the "must knows" and maybe the "should knows", discard the "could knows" for now.*

3. *Group the "must knows" under three structured headings - a) introduction, b) main body, and c) summary and close.*

"Tell them what you are going to tell them, tell them, then tell them what you've told them"

Now...

• *Consider the time available for the presentation. After all the "must knows" have been included can any of the "should knows" be added in? If so, choose the most relevant first.*

• *Group the points you have decided to include under subject headings but do not consider the sequence at this stage.*

• *Place the subject headings in a logical, interesting order.*

• *Put a time allocation on each subject and the use of each visual aid.*

• *Make working notes for the presentation.*

• *Prepare the introduction – what you are going to talk about and why it will be of interest to your students. How long will the presentation be and when do you want to take questions? Will you be giving them a handout or should they make their own notes. Make sure you include a statement about your objectives.*

• *Rehearse your presentation, and modify as necessary.*

• *Check that you have covered your objectives and have a way to measure that they have been achieved. If your objective was that your students would be able to don a lifejacket properly in a timely manner, then why not have them do so at the end of your presentation?*

• *Select the most relevant visual aids remembering the location for the presentation.*

• *What is Plan "B"?*

Ashore or afloat – theory or practical?

Knowing the objectives and the location will have an absolute impact on whether your session is ashore or afloat, theory or practical. Even so many of the elements of planning and preparation are the same. Consider the general anatomy of a presentation.

Start by planning the session, run the session and then consider how it went. If necessary, make a few changes to the plan, ready for next time.

Anatomy of a session

For the session itself, start by sharing the objectives with the students in the form of the introduction, or a briefing depending on the location. Subsequently, the presentation, or task, is carried out; followed by a debrief, or summary.

For anything that involves an element of participation, it would be appropriate to first demonstrate the skill and then allow the

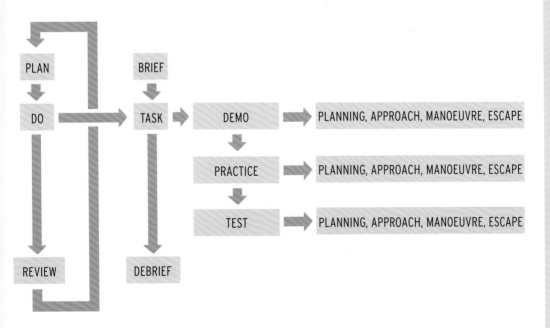

students to practice it before checking that they can do it without your assistance (the "test"). If the objectives are worded properly virtually all presentations or sessions will have a "test" element – a feature which tend to make the delivery much more interactive.

Particularly for on-the-water activities, the route of "planning, approach, manoeuvre, escape", will work well in most cases and put a framework around your session. Share this route with your students and they will think ahead when they are doing the activity!

PRESENTATION STRUCTURE

- *Tell them what you're going to tell them*
- *Tell them*
- *Then tell them what you told them.*

All presentations must be structured properly. Following the "Three Step Plan" you'll already have a simple structure consisting of an "introduction", a "main body", and a "summary and close". However, the structure of presentations deserves more discussion. A good presentation or session has three parts:

Introduction

The introduction should take a maximum of 10% of the total presentation time. It should include five areas:

- *What* we are going to talk about or do
- *What* we are going to do with it
- *Why* we are doing it
- *What* is the relevance of what we are doing, Safety considerations.
- *Interest* - Attention needs to be gained from the outset.
- *Need to know* - Your students must have a clear idea of why they need to know what you are going to tell them and what they are going to get out of it.
- *Title* - What is the subject matter of the presentation?
- *Scope* - What is to be covered? Do your students need to take notes or will you provide a handout?
- *Objectives* - State the level of knowledge your students will have at the end of the presentation using a statement such as "By the end of this presentation you will be able to ...". As we've seen before, our objectives need to be worded carefully so that we can measure whether they have been achieved.

Essentially, in the opening you have to "sell" your students why they will want to listen to you. You could almost consider yourself

Remember the 10 percent rule for the introduction; you must give your students enough clues to help them realise what's important about your presentation. This does not mean you save the best for your very last sentence. It means you let them know up front - share the agenda!

as a door-step salesperson. After the door is opened, you have a very short period of time to gain the interest of your "client" before the door gets shut and your opportunity to put across your message is lost!

Main Body

The main body of the presentation which contains your essential message should take around 80% of the total presentation time. For a teaching scenario this should include:

1. *Explanation – An explanation of what needs to be done or where to get information from e.g. a weather forecast*

2. *Demonstration - "This is how it's done"*

3. *Imitation - Your students collectively imitate what you have demonstrated with assistance as needed.*

4. *Practice - Allow time for your students to practice their new skills in small groups or individually. Check on progress as needed.*

For a more formal lecture scenario, the "explanation" is likely to be much the same but the remaining stages may be replaced by "This is the way it is".

Summary/Close

The final part of the presentation will take the remaining 10% of the time available and should consist of:

1. *Summary - A short recap of the material covered emphasising the key points. It must be brief and not contain any new material.*

2. *Questions - from your students to clarify their understanding.*

3. *Link - A link into any subsequent presentation or other material on this subject. Something to look forward to?*

The summary should consist of something more than a shrug of the shoulders and the comment **"And that's about it really"**!

Questions and Handouts

At the outset your presentation should state whether questions are welcome or not. Frequently, you may wish to say "I'll be pleased to take any questions at the end of the presentation" - particularly if you don't wish to be stopped whilst in full flow. Alternatively, you may prefer to answer questions as they occur to your students. If you are going to give a handout at the end, tell your students. Then they will listen to you rather than try to write down everything you say. To encourage questions, you could include in your introduction to your students that the only silly question is the one they don't ask!

Handling Questions

If a question is relevant to the presentation it deserves an answer. However, you will have to decide quite quickly whether a question is relevant. If it is not, then do not allow your presentation to be side-tracked, but suggest to the student that they see you at the end of the presentation about this topic or question. If the question is relevant, you have some opportunities depending on the purpose of your presentation. The more you know about a topic, the easier it is to get side-tracked!

One way to deal with a question may be to return the question to the rest of your students to answer. If no-one can answer it, have you taught this yet or have you taught it properly? Have you incorrectly assumed prior knowledge?

For relevant questions always provide the answer. The exception to this would be that in doing so you will cause confusion, or you will soon be coming to the part of your presentation where this is answered anyway. Above all else, if you don't know the answer, don't try to bluff. Say you are not sure and will find out and get back to them, and do just that.

QUESTIONING TECHNIQUES

If your presentation is of an interactive nature you will probably wish to ask questions of your students to test their learning. A well thought-out question, properly delivered, allows an instructor to:

• *Check that your students have understood you*

• *Keep your students involved in your session*

• *Enable the students to be a part of their learning cycle*

When asking a question the golden rule is
"POSE, PAUSE, POUNCE":

• **POSE** *the question to all the students*

• **PAUSE** *to give them time to think*

• **POUNCE** *(i.e. invite) one of them to provide an answer*

Sometimes a group may not appear to be very forthcoming with the answers to your questions. If this seems to be the case be careful that after asking a question you do not provide the answer too quickly. A long pause is often all that is required for someone to offer a suggestion.

Try not to ask questions with more than one answer, or to ask closed questions i.e. those which can be answered with a simple "yes" or "no" unless that's all you want.

THE VOICE

The voice is an important asset to an instructor and can tell your students a great deal about them. When we are speaking, only a small percentage of the emotional impact comes from the words themselves, far more important is the force, pitch and tone of the voice. For instance, when we describe someone as being "boring", we are often referring to their voice.

Force

Can the students at the back hear clearly? Are the ones at the front being deafened? It's not simply a matter of shouting, but rather a matter of projecting the voice to where it needs to be heard. If the instructor tends to shout instead of projecting their voice, using force properly, then a sore throat can easily result. Your students are unlikely to appreciate it either!

Pitch

Everyone has a natural pitch to their voice which they use in everyday speech. If you try to talk outside of this natural pitch your speech will sound very false.

Tone

An instructor can give a totally wrong impression of himself/herself by sounding angry, sarcastic or critical. The wrong tone will rapidly turn your students against you and they will stop listening to the message being put across. A good idea is to record yourself delivering a presentation. Would you like to listen to the lecture?

Accent

Do not worry if you have an accent. It is a part or what makes each of us individuals. It is only when your accent is so "local" that no-one else from outside your immediate area can understand you that it causes problems.

AFTER THE PRESENTATION

Following the "Plan, Do, Review" concept mentioned earlier, now is the time to consider how your presentation went and ask yourself if you could do anything to improve it. You could follow up your presentation by asking some of your students for feedback, either informally or by using a feedback questionnaire. Only do this if you want to receive feedback which may not be as positive as you'd hoped.

Using the feedback and your own observations you should be able to modify areas where improvement is appropriate – and retain areas that worked well.

It is becoming quite common, especially in schools and Local Authority centres, for an instructor to be "observed" during the delivery of a session. This may be a part of an annual review process, or simply a quality control mechanism. Such observations should be regarded as a positive exercise. Listen to the feedback you receive and act on it!

PLAN

DO

REVIEW

VISUAL AIDS

Anything which is used to support your "lesson" should do just that. It should not be a demonstration of your own battle with technology, even if you stand a good chance of success. Adopt the KISS approach - "Keep It Simple - Stupid"!

The visual aid most appropriate for your presentation will depend entirely on its purpose and your students. A variety of visual aids are discussed on the following pages.

Every presentation uses visual aids in some way, even if the only visual aid is the instructor himself. For some presentations this may be the best or most appropriate visual aid. For many presentations, however, there is an absolute need to describe a point with a diagram or a model.

How and when are visual aids best used?

Definition

We can call a visual aid anything your students can see (or hear) that helps you get their message across. While this definition sounds simple, it provides a foundation to measure the effectiveness of visual aids. You should always ask yourself these two questions when using visuals:

• *Will your students be able to see the visual aid?*
• *Will the visual aid help get a point across more clearly?*

If the answer is not a definite YES, the visual should not be used because it will detract from your presentation rather than support it.

Consider using a visual aid ONLY when it will help your students to VISUALISE something you are talking about, or to SUMMARISE your points.

We have all seen overhead projector foils which the instructor simply reads. This visual aid abuse adds nothing to the presentation and in fact detracts from it. Your students will read ahead and ignore any useful comments you might make.

Models are great - unless they are fragile. Comments such as "And this bit used to go on here" don't help a presentation unless it's about fixing broken models!

Visual Aids Use

Before using ANY form of visual aid consider what you want it to achieve and don't try to use something just because it's available! Follow the KISS principle here too.

"A picture speaks a thousand words" - use a visual aid and shut up!"

Is it needed? *Do not use a visual aid simply because you've seen other people use it. Any visual aids must serve a purpose and be applicable to that specific subject.*

Is it simple? *The more complicated the visual aid the more chance there is that it will go wrong or the instructor will have problems using it. Two simple visual aids that work are better than one which does not.*

Make it reusable *If time and effort has been put into making a visual aid, it should be reusable.*

Practice *Practice using a visual aid before you use it for the first time. This will avoid problems such as finding the on/off switch on the OHP.*

Do not trust technology *If you are using technology, make sure you have a "plan B" in case it fails or is not available.*

And *Only have a visual aid on show whilst it is being used. Your students will be intrigued by a model for some time before you refer to it. OHP's should be "off" unless a slide is actually being referred to.*

Visual aids need to enhance your presentation and not simply repeat what you are saying. Whilst the visual aids may provide a framework for your ideas, try to avoid using them to remind you what you should be mentioning next. You still need your notes.

Making Visual Aids Work

What is your first thought when asked to give a presentation? You may have started by producing OHP foils or your PC based presentation. However, this approach will have your visual aids driving your presentation rather than the other way around.

"Avoid the temptation to use a visual aid just because it's available"

The quality and simplicity of visual aids is vital. Correct use of visual aids will grab the students' attention and focus it on the important points. So start with the presentation plan and THEN see where a visual aid might assist.

Your students will expect professional quality visual aids. After all, you are a professional. The following sections are designed to help you use and develop effective visual aids in your presentation.

Reality

In a perfect world, your students would always understand what you mean - even if it is not entirely clear. Your visual aids support what you say and can actually be more important. Visual aids will most likely use the students' eyes, so design them by looking at them from the students' perspective.

What does this mean? Can your visual aid be seen from where your students will be sitting? If you don't know, sit there and see for yourself. Having considered whether the visual aid can be seen, how complicated is it? The human brain is very complex but cannot do too many things at once!

A good presentation slide should be clear, concise and easily understood

Put no more than five or six items on an OHP foil or PC screen. Ideally just put a picture and a heading. Does it pass the t-shirt test? Would your image look reasonable on the back of a t-shirt and can you read it?

Don't put long involved descriptions on your visual aids.
Your students will simply be reading what you have written rather than listening to you.

Make your objectives apparent to your students so they can understand how the visual aid is relevant.

The "easy rule"

You don't have long to give your students the benefit of your experience. Your message may be quite complicated, but your visual aids are there to make it easy on your students: easy on their eyes, easy to understand, and easy to remember. If you follow the easy rule, your students will have no trouble understanding what you are trying to teach them.

VISUAL AIDS SELECTION

There are many different types of visual aid and all have advantages and disadvantages. In this section we will consider some of the more common ones and how they can be used to good advantage.

The object itself

The object itself is often overlooked as a visual aid. Sometimes, a discussion of the safety equipment to carry on a powerboat involves lists on a board and perhaps photographs. Instead, why not have your students find the various items of safety equipment carried on the powerboat you are going to use? Suddenly, the "lecture" becomes a practical session with actual equipment being used. It's more hands-on and every item is, hopefully, in situ, rather than in a photograph.

If you cannot avoid using something other than the object itself, or the session does not fit into something that could be made practical, here are some guidelines:

Data Projector

If you know how to use the equipment, presentations can be significantly enhanced through this modern technology. However, the equipment is expensive and it is vital that the instructor is 100% familiar with its operation. Without this level of familiarity, this form of delivery can become more of a distraction, or source of entertainment to your students, than an asset. Despite the cost issues, data projectors allow very flexible presentations and it is possible to include video clips within conventional slides. A big tip – avoid using all the whizzy effects which serve only to be visual distractions.

Chalkboard

Usually called the blackboard but political correctness now dictates that they are called chalkboards. There are perceived health issues over the chalk dust and very few of these still exist, having been replaced with "dry-wipe" boards which are rather more flexible.

Whiteboard/Dry Wipe Board

The whiteboard or dry wipe board is probably the most common, most flexible, least technological visual aid. Some even have a magnetic surface. But they are only of any use if your writing or diagrams can be seen or understood by your students. Your words or diagrams need to be planned so that the board does not become a note-pad for your random thoughts!

Overhead Projector (OHP)

Although many are simply to use, modern portable versions frequently require considerable manual dexterity skills to set up. The OHP is one of the most abused pieces of visual aid equipment. Not only does it have a trip hazard across the room, many users turn away from their students' to read from the screen. To control the focus of your students' attention on you or the screen you

"Remember that the OHP does have an "off" switch - use it from time to time"

can easily use the off switch. We cannot leave the topic of OHP without considering the design of slides. Make the writing large enough for your students to read easily. A rule of no more than 20 words per slide will encourage a decent letter size.

Slide Projector

A darkened room is required and the slides need to be good quality. Unless you are delivering your talk to a very large group you would be better advised to get prints of the slides and use those instead. Images could be scanned and used in a PC based presentation.

Flip Charts

Flip charts can be a very useful way to collect ideas from your students and then retain them as a list on the wall. It's a bit like the dry wipe board but without the need to wipe it. A stand is usually required to hold the flip chart paper - take care not to trip over the legs! Finally, make sure you have enough paper before you start.

Models

Models can be particularly useful when it is not practical to use the real thing. However, don't make them too complicated. Make them easy to replace when, not if, they break. If the real thing is available use it and forget the model. A cut out model can show how a piece of equipment works but it may be difficult to position so all your students can see.

Video Tapes

A video player and TV are needed – as is the knowledge of how to use them. Don't let your group of young people be the ones to show you how it works! Problems can occur when you want to use just one part of the video and you will need to set the tape to the correct starting point before your students arrive.

Handouts:

- *For visual variety, why not provide handouts on pale yellow or blue paper?*
- *Is there a corporate image for all handouts used at your centre?*
- *Distribute the handouts just prior to discussing the topics.*
- *Have extra handouts for unexpected participants.*
- *Keep one for yourself so questions on your handout can be answered easily.*

For all visual aids ... remember!!!

• *Always be prepared to change your visual aids or consider whether they actually add anything to your presentation.*

• *Make certain that your presentation directs the visual aids, not the other way around.*

More on the Data Projector and Overhead Projector

The data projector and overhead projector are the most used, and frequently abused, of all visual aids. It seems that everyone in business has one and regularly uses it. They are now common fixtures in many RYA training centres and can greatly enhance your presentation if they are used correctly. They are generally easy to use and can accommodate large or small groups of students.

"For powerboating, why not use a powerboat as a visual aid?

Some tips on using the OHP or data projector:

Pre-Presentation Checks:

Projector:

- *Make sure you know how it works*
- *On/Off switch*
- *Lamp changeover (for an OHP)*
- *Focus control*
- *Check it works*
- *The position of mains lead should comply with health and safety requirements*
- *How does the laptop PC interface with the projector?*

OHP foils:

- *Make sure the foils are in the correct order*

Keystone Effect

When an image is projected onto a screen it may appear as a wedge shape. This is known as the "keystone effect" because of it's shape and it occurs when the projector, or OHP's projection head, is not aligned exactly with the screen. The result is a distorted image and it may also be difficult to focus the entire image. Data projectors usually provide a way for this distortion to be corrected, for an OHP you may need to move it or the alignment of the screen. Set this up before the students arrive.

Focusing

Make sure that the image is properly focused. A blurred image is difficult to read and does bring into question the instructor's preparation and professionalism. Do this before the students arrive.

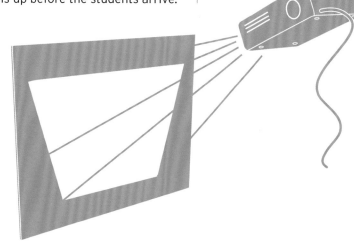

Checklist:

- Make sure the plug reaches the socket without trying to stretch it
  - Think safe!
- Can everyone see the screen?
- Put the projector at a height that is comfortable for you
- Make sure the lens is dust free
- Put the projector on a vibration free base
- Focus and centre the picture on the screen beforehand
- If you are using an OHP, number your foils and check that they are in the right order and the right way around
- Never assume your projector will work. Have a plan "B" ready!

During Presentations:

- Make sure you are not blocking anyone's view of the screen
- Darken the room if needed
- To control the attention of your students switch the projector off when you are not using it for more than a couple of minutes
- Talk to your students, not to the screen. If you've set it up correctly, the image on the screen will be like the one on the PC screen or OHP in front of you!
- Use a pointer to emphasise points

Designing OHP Foils and screens for data projectors.

The elements of design for both OHP foils and data projector screens are essentially the same. The data projector is rather more flexible in terms of what can be included and, of course, providing you know how to use the software, the screens are easy to modify and update.

"Above all, remember ... Keep It Large and Legible (KILL)"

Most screens are more inclined to a landscape format but if that does not work well you may need to use a portrait format for your presentation. Whichever you use make it the same for all slides in the presentation. Key points to bear in mind:

- Slides should have a title
- Does each slide make a point?

- *Use a balance of words and graphics*
- *No more than 20 words per screen*
- *Use a consistent typeface*
- *Use a type size that is large enough to be read from the back of the room*
- *Fill the screen*

So... if our presentation were on slide design, and our key message were the points noted above ... what would our slide look like? There are several options. One option could be a simple list, the other could be a graphic.

Whatever means you use to deliver your presentation, are you capable of using the equipment? If not, try something else. It will be a source of much amusement to your students to see you struggle with technology. Your lesson will certainly be memorable but will your students have learnt what you intended, or the fact that you cannot use a laptop PC?

"Your slide supports your message – it does not give it!"

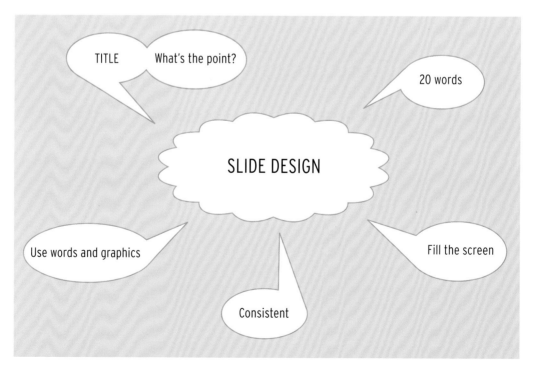

PRESENTATION SKILLS AND THE RYA POWERBOAT COURSE

It would be pointless to discuss, in depth, strategies to enable the instructor to deliver a session without providing a link to the skills the instructor actually has to cover. In the next section we will look at the skills involved and how to teach them, but what is the standard, what is the teaching emphasis?

"Too much to teach in just two days" is one of the most common criticisms made by instructors of the existing Powerboat syllabus. How can we teach all of these subjects within the allocated time?

To address this, all subjects in the powerboating schemes have been assigned to three different levels of teaching.

These three levels are:

1. The student has A KNOWLEDGE OF the subject.

The subject will be briefly explained, and the student knows where to find out further information at a later date.

An example taken from Level 2 would be Hull Types. Explain the characteristics of the hull of the vessel that is being used for the course and then point the student in the direction of further sources of information, such as the RYA Start Powerboating or RYA Powerboat Handbook.

2. The student UNDERSTANDS the subject.

The subject has been covered in greater depth and the student has demonstrated a basic understanding and will be able to go away from the course and further develop their own skill in this area. Confirmation of the student's understanding of the subject could be achieved in a number of ways, maybe a short quiz near the end of the course.

An example taken from Level 2 would be Distress Signals and the Mayday Call. This session would include an explanation of the use of flares and a description of the correct mayday procedure. A student attending a VHF SRC course at a later date would achieve further learning on this subject.

3. The student CAN demonstrate a level of proficiency in the subject.

The subject has been covered in great depth, including background theory, practical demonstrations by the instructor and practice by the student until they can demonstrate sound skills in this subject.

An example taken from Level 2 would be IRPCS. At the end of the course the student can explain and demonstrate the correct action to be taken to avoid collisions with other craft, principally rules 5, 7, 8, 9, 12-19.

Another example from Level 2 would be mooring alongside. At the end of the course the student can demonstrate mooring alongside a pontoon or moored craft, taking into account both wind and, where applicable, tide.

ASSESSMENT METHOD

Before moving on we need to consider how we are going to assess our students' ability and progress. Even if you follow every guideline here, different students will progress at different rates and achieve different levels of competence.

"Competence" gives us a clue as to how to assess a student. Some further ideas for this are included later when we look at the content of each course - for now we have to consider that the assessment method must be shared with the students during the welcome and introduction session of their course.

Will there be an exam or is assessment continuous? What is the standard required - can they make mistakes? It is essential that you avoid turning any course into a two day exam with feedback only at the end - and the students unaware of what boxes have been ticked until that time.

If you think that you need to use an exam you should have a very clear idea as to what it is supposed to demonstrate and what the pass mark is. If a student achieves 1% below your pass mark have they passed the course? If so then the "pass mark" is nothing of

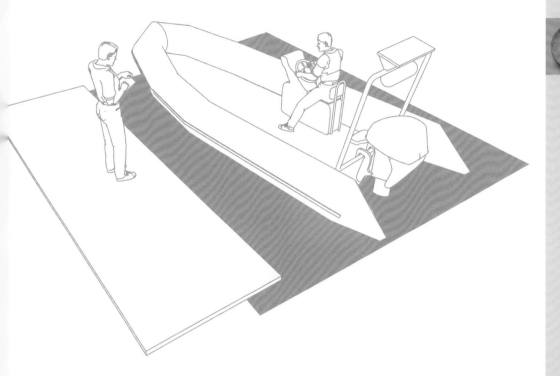

the sort! In using an exam you will additionally need to consider whether your students can read or understand the questions?

Why not consider how else you can establish your students' understanding of what you have taught them. One alternative to an exam could be to ask the students questions as you progress through the course?

All your students need to be treated equally and your standard needs to be substantially the same as other RYA Powerboat Training Centres.

Of help in assessing this standard will be:

- *The checklist and standards required for a Level 2 Direct Assessment shown later in this handbook. The end result of a Level 2 course or a Direct Assessment should be the same, so it follows that the same minimum standards should have been achieved.*
- *The lesson/sessions plans for each course.*

In assessing your students' ability you must remember that not everyone will pass a Level 2 (for instance) course in two days. Sometimes, a student will need a little more time to consolidate their new-found skills or, perhaps, weather conditions prevented much time afloat. Whatever the reason for not satisfactorily completing some parts of the syllabus, always remember that RYA powerboat course certificates are awarded for achievement - not for attendance! If your course introduction includes a statement on the assessment method that will be used, and the possible course outcomes, subsequently discussing slow progress or poor performance becomes much easier.

Practical skills are often harder to assess so some additional guidance may assist new or inexperienced instructors. Here we will consider a session involving securing to a mooring on a Level 2 course:

SESSION **09**

LEAVING AND COMING ALONGSIDE:

AIM: Be able to demonstrate a good approach to and departure from a jetty or pontoon, correct angle and speed, escape route, communication and brief crew, use springs.

LEVEL 1: KNOWLEDGE OF
LEVEL 2: UNDERSTANDS
· Approach into strongest element
· Communicate to crew their action on arrival and departure

LEVEL 1: UNDERSTANDS
· Use springs to bring stern off jetty
LEVEL 2: CAN
· Assess angle and speed of approach
· Make fast alongside

FUNDAMENTALS:
○ Identify an escape route
○ Prepare warps ready for arrival
○ Brief crew and confirm understanding

ABOARD
○ ○ ○

ASHORE
○ ○

THEORY
○ ○

CONSIDERATIONS FOR LESSON PLANS:
· Maintain all round look out for other water users
· Shallow angle on approach, minimum speed, prepare lines
· Check lines are secured in boat prior to securing ashore

DISPLACEMENT BOAT:
· Remember to use fenders if required
· May want to use a spring line to bring boat alongside

TILLER STEER:
· Same as RIB
Its easier to put way on, than to take way off, approach slowly, use neutral as the favoured gear

SOURCES FOR FURTHER INFORMATION: G20 G48 G13

SESSION **09**

RIB ARRIVING AT A PONTEEN

COMMANDO DEPARTING

Starting with these criteria, did the student read the wind and tide correctly? Was the speed of the boat controlled? Was the boat effectively secured to the buoy? Naturally, an element of consistency is required so during a course the student should be given more than one attempt to demonstrate that they can achieve this. Similarly, if they get it wrong they may need appropriate feedback followed by more practice.

If you consider that a student is falling short of the standard required there are a number of things to consider:

- *The student needs to know early so that they have a chance to do something about it.*
- *Is it the student's inability to learn or your teaching?*
- *What is the action plan that will be shared with the student giving guidance on what you and he/she can do to reach a more appropriate standard?*

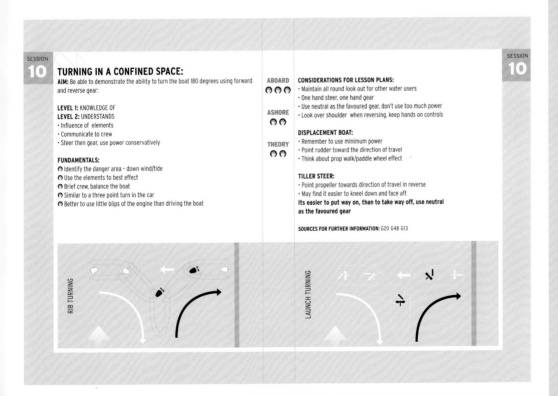

SESSION 10

TURNING IN A CONFINED SPACE:

AIM: Be able to demonstrate the ability to turn the boat 180 degrees using forward and reverse gear:

LEVEL 1: KNOWLEDGE OF
LEVEL 2: UNDERSTANDS
- Influence of elements
- Communicate to crew
- Steer then gear, use power conservatively

FUNDAMENTALS:
- ⟳ Identify the danger area - down wind/tide
- ⟳ Use the elements to best effect
- ⟳ Brief crew, balance the boat
- ⟳ Similar to a three point turn in the car
- ⟳ Better to use little blips of the engine than driving the boat

ABOARD
⟳ ⟳ ⟳

ASHORE
⟳ ⟳

THEORY
⟳ ⟳

CONSIDERATIONS FOR LESSON PLANS:
- Maintain all round look out for other water users
- One hand steer, one hand gear
- Use neutral as the favoured gear, don't use too much power
- Look over shoulder when reversing, keep hands on controls

DISPLACEMENT BOAT:
- Remember to use minimum power
- Point rudder toward the direction of travel
- Think about prop walk/paddle wheel effect

TILLER STEER:
- Point propeller towards direction of travel in reverse
- May find it easier to kneel down and face aft
- **Its easier to put way on, than to take way off, use neutral as the favoured gear**

SOURCES FOR FURTHER INFORMATION: G20 G48 G13

RIB TURNING

LAUNCH TURNING

DEVELOPING A PRESENTATION OR LESSON PLAN

All of the foregoing will have been wasted if the instructor cannot pull everything together to form a structured lesson. In this section we will develop the outline of a lesson plan. In particular we will consider a session to deliver a ten minute presentation on a Level 2 Powerboat Course for "Sources of weather information".

Later in this handbook you will find the Powerboat Method where Session 16 outlines the scope of what needs to be covered. The relevant section is duplicated below:

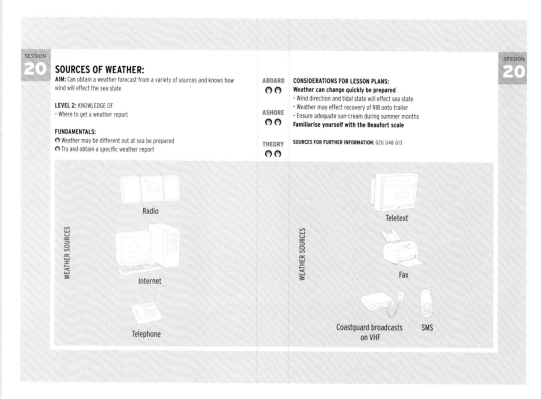

This clearly provides the session aims, where to get background information, if required, and some considerations for the lesson plan. A lesson delivery suggestion; since day two of the course at a coastal venue typically involves a passage, it makes sense to have the students get a forecast themselves. This can be given as "homework" at the end of Day 1, and which can then be discussed at the beginning of day 2, bringing out the points noted above in relation to the passage about to be undertaken. Further required teaching points can be brought in from "what if" questions. This provides an outline of our lesson but we need to plan a bit more.

The first part of the plan is to consider the objectives and aims. You can see this in the session outline above. How this can best be achieved will vary from session to session and in this example, to make our session less formal, we will adopt a style of a discussion rather than a lecture. Note that this session contains theory that should wherever possible be covered on the boat or ashore.

Next, look at the suggested resources as these will provide ideas on what to include, as well as diagrams to help you explain the topic.

Start by getting the students to state where they have got their forecasts from and where they would normally get a forecast when they are at home. They should be able to get a list of ten or more which can then be discussed with reference to currency (how up-to-date), availability and cost. We specifically want to include "looking out of the window", as well as any other good local sources.

Having considered the sources, we can consider what the forecast tells us and how it may affect our passage. "What if" scenarios could be used as appropriate. For example, if we launch from a slipway onto a calm sea, how might recovery of the RIB be affected by an increasing on-shore breeze?

The lesson plan needs to include a "need to know" and the specific learning objectives. These aspects are a part of the introduction. Imagine you are a doorstep salesperson selling your presentation. You have the length of your introduction (say less than one minute) to sell the "need to know" to your audience before they close the door! In that one minute you also need to state your specific objectives.

With the need to know and objectives set we also have also

provided the scope of the summary in the form of a recap of the areas covered and a measure of student knowledge in the form of questions and answers.

The body of the session in this case is a discussion which generally requires the instructor to have a very good knowledge of the subject and good resources to fully understand input from the students. In the case of weather information sources, students may suggest VHF radio, NAVTEX or Metfax, etc. The instructor needs to have a working knowledge of these. The objectives from the introduction will help to keep your content within scope. For instance, in this case the interpretation of a weather (synoptic) chart is out of scope and should not be covered.

The plan needs some timings so that the pace of delivery is consistent throughout. The implications in this case are that there needs to be some time allocated for gathering the sources from the students and some time for discussing them.

Before delivering the presentation, you need to check that it meets the required aims and objectives of the session and, ideally, you need to have run through the presentation at least once to check timings and that your resources and visual aids work together with your commentary.

Next, consider the location for the presentation. This particular session is intended to be theory, but does not need to be in a classroom. Consider the alternative of looking at a weather forecast in a marina office window, or sitting in the RIB looking at weather forecasts.

04

THE POWERBOATING METHOD

LEVEL 1 AND 2

CLOTHING AND BUOYANCY:

AIM: To explain the safety equipment for the boat and individual, and protection against the elements.

LEVEL 1: UNDERSTANDS

LEVEL 2: CAN
- Protect against the elements – hot and cold
- Life jacket/buoyancy aid – suitability and serviceability

FUNDAMENTALS:
- Layers or sun cream
- Wear protective clothing for heat and shade
- Personal buoyancy appropriate, in date and worn correctly

ABOARD

ASHORE

THEORY

CONSIDERATIONS FOR LESSON PLANS:

Warm clothing, wetsuit, dry suit, waterproofs, footwear
- Consider "chill factor", weather may change
- Consider effects of sun – wind can take the heat out
- Stow spare gear in watertight compartment or container
- Get weather report

DISPLACEMENT BOAT:
- No differences

TILLER STEER:
- No differences

SOURCES FOR FURTHER INFORMATION: G20 G48 G13

BUOYANCY AIDS

INTRODUCTION TO THE BOAT:

AIM: To demonstrate the equipment which should be carried on any boat to make it effective to carry out its role

LEVEL 1: UNDERSTANDS

LEVEL 2: CAN
- Boat buoyancy
- Ancillary and all safety items
- Fuel (including spare)

LEVEL 1: CAN
- Stow an anchor
- Fasten to a cleat

FUNDAMENTALS:
- Kill cord, correct length, works and spare carried
- Know how to use emergency equipment
- Check length of painter
- Ensure winch is serviceable on trailer

CONSIDERATIONS FOR LESSON PLANS:

Involve students and keep explanations brief
- Secure anchor the boat
- Check CE plate for maximum loading (number and weight)
- Fuel cells secured in boat (where fitted)

DISPLACEMENT BOAT:
- Check and pump bilges where fitted
- Additional equipment (boarding ladders, boat hook)

TILLER STEER/MANUAL TILT:
- Same as RIB
- Check engine shallow drive mechanism

Start at the front of the boat and work towards the stern

SOURCES FOR FURTHER INFORMATION: G20 G48 G13

ABOARD

ASHORE

THEORY

INTRODUCTION

RUNNING UP ENGINE:

AIM: Be able to start and stop engine safely and be aware of the importance of the kill-cord at all times

LEVEL 1: UNDERSTANDS

LEVEL 2: CAN
- Use muffs ashore if possible to warm engine, Kill-cord fitted and checked
- Prime fuel with fuel bulb
- Communication before starting and stopping engine

FUNDAMENTALS:
🕐 Try to run up engine prior to launch but definitely before you release it if possible
🕐 Use choke when required (manual or automatic)
🕐 Check all oil levels on all types of engines
🕐 Check water separator where fitted
🕐 Check tell-tale for water flow through engine

CONSIDERATIONS FOR LESSON PLANS:

Involve students and check understanding at all levels
- Wear kill-cord around leg when afloat
- Ensure gear is in neutral before starting
- Check fuel cell vents are open if fitted

DISPLACEMENT BOAT:
- Use engine de-compression to start engine
- Keep thumbs to side if using starting handle
- Check stop mechanism is in run position
- Run bilge extractor fan where fitted

TILLER/MANUAL START:
- Check behind you before pulling the hand start
- Take up slack in start rope before pulling
- Slowly return start rope to original position

SOURCES FOR FURTHER INFORMATION: G20 G48 G13

ABOARD

ASHORE 🕐 🕐 🕐

THEORY

CORRECTLY USED KILL-CORD

BOAT BEING STARTED UP

LAUNCHING AND RECOVERY:

AIM: Be able to launch and recover a boat off and on to a trailer safely and be aware of slipway dangers

LEVEL 1: KNOWLEDGE OF - (8-11 YEAR OLDS WATCH)

LEVEL 2: KNOWLEDGE OF - (12-16 YEAR OLDS ENDORSED)

· Condition of slip, width and surface

· Hazards, other water users

· State of tide and waves

LEVEL 1: CAN

· Fasten to a cleat

· Stow an anchor

LEVEL 2: CAN

· Prepare the boat for launch and secure equipment

FUNDAMENTALS:

☾ Float boat off trailer and on again when recovering

☾ Use rope between car and trailer if required

RIB BEING LAUNCHED

ABOARD ☾ ☾ ☾

☾ Ensure engine is raised prior to launch

☾ Communication at all times

ASHORE ☾ ☾

CONSIDERATIONS FOR LESSON PLANS:

Introduce knots early and build knowledge gradually

· Remove trailer board and all straps prior to launch

· Park car and trailer properly

· Think about manual handling issues

· Stay out of the danger areas (between car and trailer)

· Check ownership of slip

THEORY ☾ ☾

DISPLACEMENT BOAT:

· Manual handling due to excessive weight of boat

TILLER STEER:

· Same as RIB

Involve the students so they gain practical experience

SOURCES FOR FURTHER INFORMATION: G20 G48 G16

ROPE CORRECTLY
FIXED TO A CLEAT

SLOW SPEED MANOEUVRES: POWERING UP/DOWN:

AIM: Be able to control the boat safely at low speed highlighting the importance of the kill-cord. Also demonstrates one hand for the steering one hand for the power and communication during all manoeuvres

LEVEL 1: KNOWLEDGE OF

LEVEL 2: CAN

· Wear the kill-cord correctly at all times when the engine is running
· One hand gear one hand steer
· Communication prior to powering up or down

FUNDAMENTALS:

🜨 Look behind before setting off
🜨 Keep all round vision at all times
🜨 Decrease speed slowly to reduce pooping
🜨 Assess balance and trim
🜨 Check engine is trimmed down
🜨 Effect of wash on other boats and water users

ABOARD
€ € €

ASHORE
€

THEORY
€ €

CONSIDERATIONS FOR LESSON PLANS:

Good demonstrations are effective but should be brief

· Steer then gear
· Gradually increase power after warning crew
· Get weight forward to assist in getting bow down
· When stopping, gradually decrease speed to avoid "pooping" and make a turn to the side

DISPLACEMENT BOAT:

· Usually slow acceleration
· Usually carries way when in neutral

TILLER STEER:

· Get weight forward to stop bow rising
· Use one hand throttle one hand holding on
· Sit opposite side to the tiller. However there may be some craft where this is not practical – Zapcat for example.

Focus on positive coaching, giving a clear picture
SOURCES FOR FURTHER INFORMATION: G20 G48 G16

CORRECT WEARING OF
KILL-CORD – TILLER STEER

CORRECT WEARING OF
KILL-CORD – RIB

REVERSING:

AIM: Be able to control the boat in reverse focusing on balance to reduce "swamping" – All round vision and communication, introduce "pivot points"

LEVEL 1: UNDERSTANDS

LEVEL 2: CAN

- Alter boat balance. Consider moving crew weight forward to lift stern
- Look all round but especially behind over your shoulder
- Point engine in direction you wish to travel

FUNDAMENTALS:

 Keep checking forward for swing of sponsons

 Pivot point (moves aft)

 Keep engine revs and speed low

 Communicate prior to each manoeuvre

 Keep all round vision

ABOARD

ASHORE

THEORY

CONSIDERATIONS FOR LESSON PLANS:

Pivot point moves closer to the transom when going astern

- Keep speed slow to reduce "swamping"
- Look over your shoulder in direction of travel

DISPLACEMENT:

- Face aft and point rudder to direction of travel
- Keep engine revs low and hold tiller tight
- Watch the swing on the bow
- Make small rudder movements
- Be aware of cross winds

TILLER:

- Same as rib
- Forward hand steer, back hand gear, face aft
- Ensure engine is locked down prior to reversing
- Consider kneeling facing backwards if practicable

Moving weight forward, lifts the stern, reduces swamping

SOURCES FOR FURTHER INFORMATION: G20 G48 G13

BOAT BEING REVERSED

BOAT BEING REVERSED

"U" "S" AND "FIGURE 8" TURNS AT SLOW SPEED, IN FORWARDS AND REVERSE:

AIM: Be able to demonstrate correct use of kill-cord, one hand steer and one hand gear. Controlled speed and control of boat, including pivot points. Communication and keeping an all round look out.

LEVEL 1:

LEVEL 2:

- Communication - important to warn crew at all times
- One hand steer, one hand gear
- All round vision looking over shoulder when reversing
- Displacement speed - under control - safety first

FUNDAMENTALS:

☾ Look prior to turn and warn crew which direction you intend to turn

☾ Check balance and trim are correct when going in reverse

☾ Check speed to reduce swamping and pooping

☾ Ensure engine is trimmed down

ONE HAND STEER AND ONE HAND GEAR

ABOARD ☾ ☾ ☾

ASHORE ☾ ☾

THEORY ☾

CONSIDERATIONS FOR LESSON PLANS:

Inform crew which way you intend to turn prior to manoeuvre

- Engine trimmed down
- When turning try turning the wheel with one hand
- Develop pivot points both in forwards and reverse

DISPLACEMENT:

- Turning circle is quite large, maintain safe speed
- Vessel carries way, reduce speed gradually in good time

TILLER:

- Same as RIB
- Balance boat using crew weight especially in reverse

Maintain a safe speed when turning and keep all round look out

SOURCES FOR FURTHER INFORMATION: G20 G48 G13

PICKING UP AND SECURING TO MOORING:

AIM: Be able to pick up a mooring, concentrating on communication, escape plan, using neutral as a gear

LEVEL 1: KNOWLEDGE OF

LEVEL 2: UNDERSTANDS

· Communicate all intentions to the crew
· Check crew understand which knot to use
· Approach against strongest element
· Approach slowly and have an escape route

LEVEL 2: CAN

· Approach and secure to buoy

FUNDAMENTALS:

🪝 Use crew to count down distance to mooring
🪝 Prepare mooring line in boat
🪝 Identify strong points for securing line in boat
🪝 Use correct knot

CONSIDERATIONS FOR LESSON PLANS:

· Secure to top of mooring buoy not tripping buoy or line
· Use round turn and two half hitches as you can undo under load either in boat or on mooring buoy
· Easier to put way on than to take way off
· Try picking up buoy at the shoulder instead of at the bow which is the highest part of the sponson

DISPLACEMENT BOAT:

· Use a boat hook for high sided vessels
· Use crew to point at the mooring when approaching
· Take a dummy run to assess elements

TILLER STEER:

· Same as RIB

Identify an escape route and make decision to abort early

SOURCES FOR FURTHER INFORMATION: G20 G48 G13

ABOARD
🪝 🪝 🪝

ASHORE
🪝 🪝

THEORY
🪝 🪝

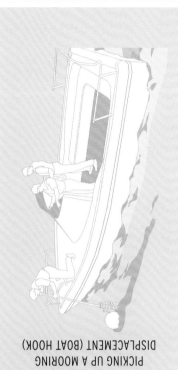

PICKING UP A MOORING
DISPLACEMENT (BOAT HOOK)

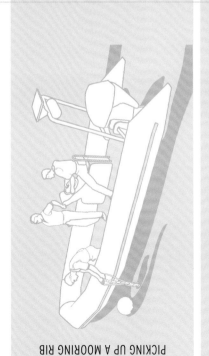

PICKING UP A MOORING RIB

LEAVING AND COMING ALONGSIDE:

AIM: Be able to demonstrate a good approach to and departure from a jetty or pontoon, correct angle and speed, escape route, communication and brief crew, use springs.

LEVEL 1: KNOWLEDGE OF

LEVEL 2: UNDERSTANDS

· Approach into strongest element

· Communicate to crew their action on arrival and departure

LEVEL 1: UNDERSTANDS

· Use springs to bring stern off jetty

LEVEL 2: CAN

· Assess angle and speed of approach

· Make fast alongside

FUNDAMENTALS:

 Identify an escape route

 Prepare warps ready for arrival

 Brief crew and confirm understanding

RIB ARRIVING AT A PONTOON

ABOARD

ASHORE

THEORY

CONSIDERATIONS FOR LESSON PLANS:

· Maintain all round look out for other water users

· Shallow angle on approach, minimum speed, prepare lines

· Check lines are secured in boat prior to securing ashore

DISPLACEMENT BOAT:

· Remember to use fenders if required

· May want to use a spring line to bring boat alongside

TILLER STEER:

· Same as RIB

Its easier to put way on, than to take way off, approach slowly, use neutral as the favoured gear

SOURCES FOR FURTHER INFORMATION: G20 G48 G13

COMMANDO DEPARTING

TURNING IN A CONFINED SPACE:

AIM: Be able to demonstrate the ability to turn the boat 180 degrees using forward and reverse gear:

LEVEL 1: KNOWLEDGE OF
LEVEL 2: UNDERSTANDS
· Influence of elements
· Communicate to crew
· Steer then gear, use power conservatively

FUNDAMENTALS:
☾ Identify the danger area – down wind/tide
☾ Use the elements to best effect
☾ Brief crew, balance the boat
☾ Similar to a three point turn in the car
☾ Better to use little blips of the engine than driving the boat

ABOARD
☾ ☾ ☾

ASHORE
☾ ☾

THEORY
☾ ☾

CONSIDERATIONS FOR LESSON PLANS:
· Maintain all round look out for other water users
· One hand steer, one hand gear
· Use neutral as the favoured gear, don't use too much power
· Look over shoulder when reversing, keep hands on controls

DISPLACEMENT BOAT:
· Remember to use minimum power
· Point rudder toward the direction of travel
· Think about prop walk/paddle wheel effect

TILLER STEER:
· Point propeller towards direction of travel in reverse
· May find it easier to kneel down and face aft
Its easier to put way on, than to take way off, use neutral as the favoured gear

SOURCES FOR FURTHER INFORMATION: G20 G48 G13

LAUNCH TURNING

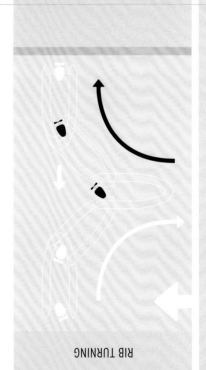

RIB TURNING

TURNING USING WARPS:

AIM: Be able to demonstrate turning the boat using warps and the engine in forwards and reverse

LEVEL 1: KNOWLEDGE OF

LEVEL 2: UNDERSTANDS

- Prepare warps and fenders if required
- Brief crew and confirm understanding
- Communication

LEVEL 2 - CAN

- Turn the boat using warps and engine using forwards and reverse gear

FUNDAMENTALS:

 Prepare warps

- Use fenders on a hard chined boat
- Use the sponsons on a RIB drive into the jetty if safe to do so
- Brief the crew and ensure hands are clear of warps and fenders etc

ABOARD

ASHORE

THEORY

CONSIDERATIONS FOR LESSON PLANS:

- Prepare warps and brief crew
- Single up the lines
- Prepare engine and assess which will be the best method - forwards or reverse

DISPLACEMENT BOAT:

- Remember to use fenders if required
- May want to walk the boat around rather than using the engine if you are trying to turn alongside

TILLER STEER:

- Same as RIB

Its easier to turn into the jetty using forwards as it takes the strain off the crew. However, reverse protects the gunnels of the boat.

SOURCES FOR FURTHER INFORMATION: G20 G48 G13

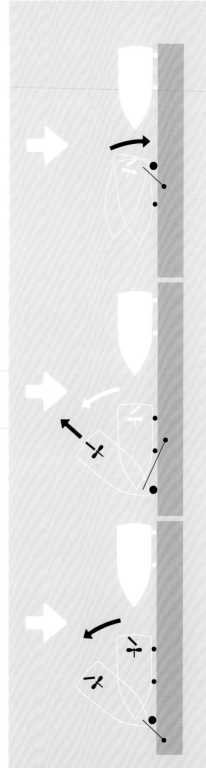

TURNING INTO A JETTY USING A RIB

PLANING SPEED:

AIM: Demonstrate a look out at all time, kill-cord, communications, one hand steer and one hand gear for control.

LEVEL 1: UNDERSTANDS
LEVEL 2: CAN
· Communicate with crew before powering up and slowing down
· Warn crew when powering up and down
· All round vision and looking behind
· One hand gear one hand steer

FUNDAMENTALS:
 Use power to break over bow wave then ease back
 Look behind before stopping, warn crew
 Stop gradually, take a gradual turn either way to stop pooping

ABOARD

ASHORE

THEORY

CONSIDERATIONS FOR LESSON PLANS:
Use the engine or transom flaps to trim the boat
· Communication at all times
· All round vision at all times
· Balance of the boat, may have to move weight forwards
· All round vision at all times
· Safe speed and think crew comfort
The position of the bow wave is a clear demonstration of when the boat is planing.

SOURCES FOR FURTHER INFORMATION: G20 G48 G13

RIB PLANING THROUGH A TURN

HIGH SPEED TURNS "U" AND "S":

AIM: Demonstrate a look out at all time, kill-cord, communications, one hand steer and one hand gear control. Introduce ventilation when turning

LEVEL 1: UNDERSTANDS

LEVEL 2: CAN

· Communicate with crew before initiating turns

· Warn crew when turning

· All round vision and looking behind

· One hand gear one hand steer

FUNDAMENTALS:

 Reduce power prior to turn

 Look around prior to turn

 Trim engine down prior to turn

 Communicate prior to turn

ABOARD

ASHORE

THEORY

CONSIDERATIONS FOR LESSON PLANS:

Use the engine or transom flaps to trim the boat

· Use waterline length when turning (trim engine down)

· Communication at all times

· All round vision at all times

· Trim engine down prior to turn to reduce the chance of ventilation

Power down, trim down, hand down... is a good order to give the students as a guide

SOURCES FOR FURTHER INFORMATION: G20 G48 G13

RIB PLANING THROUGH A TURN

TOWING AND BEING TOWED:

AIM: Is able to demonstrate how to be towed alongside and from astern

LEVEL 1: KNOWLEDGE OF
· Can accept a tow line
· Can identify strong points in the boat

LEVEL 2: UNDERSTANDS
· Communicate with other vessel and know strong points
· Knows the length of tow line in a stern tow
· Position of engine in an alongside tow

LEVEL 2: CAN
· Tie tow line into boat
· Use the correct lines for alongside tow
· Use the bridle in an astern tow

FUNDAMENTALS:
◑ Approaching the stricken vessel
◑ Setting up a tow can take a long time – assess dangers of drift in tide and wind
◑ The use of the bridle when towing astern
◑ Ensure all ropes are clear of propeller when starting and stopping

CONSIDERATIONS FOR LESSON PLANS:
Confirm signals and agree terms for salvage if required
· DO NOT BECOME A CASUALTY YOURSELF
· Length of tow line in an astern tow must be long enough
· Alongside tow all lines should be tight
· Ensure the engine of the tug is behind the transom of the tow when towing alongside

DISPLACEMENT BOAT:
· Same warps as RIB
· Assist the turning when towing alongside by using the rudder
· Use fenders when using alongside tow

TILLER STEER:
· Same as RIB
· Use fenders if hard chined boat
Raise engine and move weight into tug when towing alongside in a planning boat to reduce weight on tug
SOURCES FOR FURTHER INFORMATION: G20 G48 G13

ABOARD

ASHORE

THEORY

TOWING ALONGSIDE

Towing vessel 'angled in
Towing vessel well astern
Spring 'f' takes load in forward
Spring 'r' in astern

TOWING ASTERN

WAVELENGTH   WAVELENGTH

ANCHORING:

AIM: Is able to deploy and recover the anchor and check for holding using transits

LEVEL 2: UNDERSTANDS
· Communicate with crew and prepare anchor
· Secure bitter end to boat and lay out warp
· Use transits to check holding

LEVEL 2: KNOWLEDGE OF
· Types of anchors and stowage
· Weighing anchor

FUNDAMENTALS:
☺ Approach against strongest element
☺ Prepare anchor and warp - chain or rope
☺ Communicate with crew and select anchorage
☺ Lower anchor and drift back or use reverse

ABOARD

ASHORE ☺

THEORY ☺

CONSIDERATIONS FOR LESSON PLANS:
Use transits or compass bearing to check holding
· Pay out a minimum of 5 times depth of water for rope
· Pay out a minimum of 3 times depth of water for chain

DISPLACEMENT BOAT:
· Consider using a tripping line and buoy
· Use a boat hook when recovering the anchor

TILLER STEER:
· Same as RIB
Is the tide on the flood or the ebb? If in doubt let out.

SOURCES FOR FURTHER INFORMATION: G20 G48 G13

SCOPE THROUGH WATER,
ANCHOR LAID OUT ON SEABED

Scope

Depth

All chain length = 4 x Depth   Mixed chain & rope = 6 x Depth

DIFFERENT SORTS OF ANCHOR

CQR or Plough   Dartmouth   Bruce   Delta

Grapnell   Fishermans   Mud Anchor

MAN OVERBOARD:

AIM: Is able to return to the MOB using the correct approach, aware of misprocedure and getting person into boat

LEVEL 2: KNOWLEDGE OF
- How to recover MOB

LEVEL 2: CAN
- Turn towards the MOB and do a wide sweep, reducing speed gradually
- Approach against the wind

FUNDAMENTALS:
- As soon as contact is made turn engine off
- Turn into MOB to keep propeller away
- Crew keep watch on MOB at all times
- If you miss repeat the process
- Try pointing bow at MOB to see which direction the conditions are taking you

ABOARD

ASHORE

THEORY

CONSIDERATIONS FOR LESSON PLANS:

The technique is like picking up a mooring but without the tide
- When MOB is alongside "turn engine off"
- Create enough room to make a controlled approach
- Approach upwind and let RIB drift onto MOB

DISPLACEMENT BOAT:
- More suitable to the "drift down method" as the weather has more effect on the hull
- Use a boarding ladder if high freeboard
- If no ladder use a coil of rope

TILLER STEER:
- Same as RIB

If you fall overboard inflate lifejacket and raise arm

SOURCES FOR FURTHER INFORMATION: G20 G48 G13

MOB DRIFT DOWN

MOB APPROACHING
AGAINST WIND

IRPCS:

AIM: Is aware of the IRPCS to be a safe operator keeping a lookout at all times and making intentions clear

LEVEL 1: UNDERSTANDS

LEVEL 2: CAN
- Keep a good look out at all times
- Make your intentions clear at all times
- Maintain a safe speed

FUNDAMENTALS:
- Check for collision by using compass bearing
- When giving way, alter course or slow down or both
- Stay out of narrow channels where commercial shipping operate

ABOARD

ASHORE

THEORY

CONSIDERATIONS FOR LESSON PLANS:

RIB/Displacement boat/Tiller steer:
- Cross channel at 90 degrees when safe to do so
- Stay on starboard side of channels power passes port to port
- Overtaking boat keeps clear
- Power gives way to sail
- Head on situation both turn to starboard pass port to port
- Actions of stand on and give way vessel
- Use real situation whilst afloat to point out IRPCS

Demonstrate IRPCS afloat and consolidate ashore

SOURCES FOR FURTHER INFORMATION: G20 G48 G13

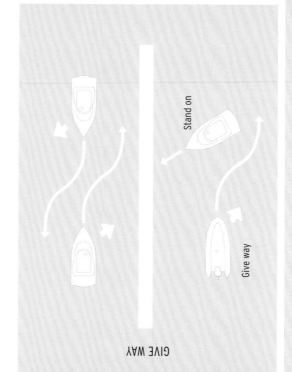

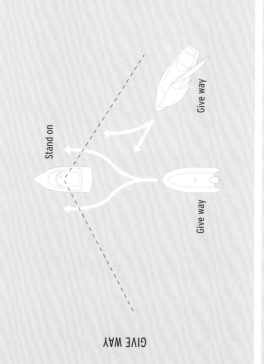

18 TYPES OF HULL AND DRIVES:

AIM: Has a knowledge of several shapes and drive types available

LEVEL 2: KNOWLEDGE OF

· Advantages of sea keeping capabilities
· Engine and drive types
· Engine maintenance
· Close down procedures

FUNDAMENTALS:

◑ Petrol and diesel, types of engines
◑ Single and twin screw

ABOARD
◑◑

ASHORE
◑◑◑

THEORY
◑

CONSIDERATIONS FOR LESSON PLANS:

Whichever boat you decide on never overload it

· Consider using different boats from around the marina

DISPLACEMENT BOAT:

· Look at planing boats

TILLER STEER:

· Same as RIB

An overloaded boat is prone to swamping.

SOURCES FOR FURTHER INFORMATION: G20 G48 G13

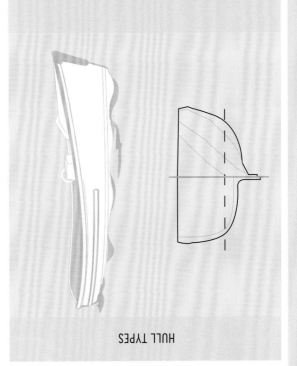

HULL TYPES

HULL TYPES

GPS:

AIM: Knows the basic functions of the GPS - Limitations and benefits

LEVEL 2 – KNOWLEDGE OF

· How to use GPS
· Benefits of GPS

FUNDAMENTALS:

☾ Line of sight navigation
☾ Relies on user programming correctly

ABOARD ☾ ☾

ASHORE ☾ ☾

THEORY ☾

CONSIDERATIONS FOR LESSON PLANS:

Use GPS to back up paper chart work but take spare batteries

· Check waypoint entry on chart
· GPS COG will make allowances for tide
· Don't rely totally on GPS

Use waterproof charts and pre-plan route

SOURCES FOR FURTHER INFORMATION: G20 G48 G13

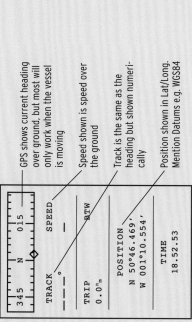

```
        ROUTE: 11
   _____
    DART TO COOMBE
   _____
 NO WAYPOINT BTW DTW
  1 DARMOU    138° 4.6
  2 N COOM        °  .
  3  _ _ _ _ _   °  .
  4  _ _ _ _ _   °  .
  5  _ _ _ _ _   °  .
   _____
    TOTAL DST   4.58
      COPY TO: _
     CLR? INV? ACT?
```

Bearing from GPS is the same as the chart

Distance from GPS is the same as the chart

GPS shows current heading over ground, but most will only work when the vessel is moving

Speed shown is speed over the ground

Track is the same as the heading but shown numerically

Position shown in Lat/Long. Mention Datums e.g. WGS84

```
  _____
 |  345    N    015  |
 |       ___◇___     |
 |    _ _ °          |
 | TRACK    SPEED    |
 |   °       |       |
 |                   |
 | TRIP     BTW      |
 | 0.0ⁿ      |       |
 |                   |
 |    POSITION       |
 |  N 50°46.469'     |
 |  W 001°10.554'    |
 |                   |
 |     TIME          |
 |   18.52.53        |
  _____
```

BTW - The bearing of one waypoint from another (usually the next one on your route)
DTW - The distance of one waypoint from another (usually the next one on your route)
COG - Course over the ground after tide and leeway
SOG - Speed over the ground after influence
XTE - Cross track error - how much you have deviated from the direct route when travelling between two waypoints

USING GPS

SESSION

20

SOURCES OF WEATHER:

AIM: Can obtain a weather forecast from a variety of sources and knows how wind will effect the sea state

LEVEL 2: KNOWLEDGE OF
- Where to get a weather report

FUNDAMENTALS:
€ Weather may be different out at sea–be prepared
€ Try and obtain a specific weather report

ABOARD
€ €

ASHORE
€ €

THEORY
€ €

CONSIDERATIONS FOR LESSON PLANS:

Weather can change quickly be prepared
- Wind direction and tidal state will effect sea state
- Weather may effect recovery of RIB onto trailer
- Ensure adequate sun-cream during summer months

Familiarise yourself with the Beaufort scale

SOURCES FOR FURTHER INFORMATION: G20 G48 G13

Teletext

Fax

SMS

Coastguard broadcasts on VHF

WEATHER SOURCES

Radio

Internet

Telephone

WEATHER SOURCES

EMERGENCY SITUATIONS:

AIM: How to cope with a fire, how to attract attention and make a mayday call

LEVEL 2: UNDERSTANDS
· Emergency actions to prevent sinking
· Alternative means of propulsion
· Fire fighting
· Mayday call

FUNDAMENTALS:
☾ Always carry an anchor
☾ Always carry flares and fire extinguisher
☾ Have an alternative means of propulsion
☾ Know international signs for distress

ABOARD
☾ ☾ ☾

ASHORE
☾ ☾

THEORY
☾

CONSIDERATIONS FOR LESSON PLANS:

ATTEND A RYA VHF DSC COURSE SO YOU CAN USE THE RADIO
· Adequate engine maintenance ensures reliability
· Flares should be in date and readily accessible
· Learn the international distress signals
· Don't smoke if fuel is petrol
· Ensure correct type of extinguisher (CO_2, powder or foam)
Fire triangle – Air, Fuel, Heat – Don't smoke onboard

SOURCES FOR FURTHER INFORMATION: G20 G48 G13

EMERGENCY EQUIPMENT

22 THEORY: BUOYAGE IALA:

AIM: Be able to demonstrate a

LEVEL 1: KNOWLEDGE OF
- IALA lateral channel markers

LEVEL 2: UNDERSTANDS
- Cardinal marks – shape and colour
- Lateral channel markers
- Other marks

LEVEL 1: UNDERSTANDS
- Cardinal marks

LEVEL 2: CAN
- Use IALA as a means to navigation

FUNDAMENTALS:
- ☾ Cardinal shape and colour
- ☾ Lateral channel marks shape and colour
- ☾ Special marks, isolated danger and preferred channel markers

CONSIDERATIONS FOR LESSON PLANS:
- Show on the water and consolidate back ashore if required
- Show as many different marks on the water as possible

It is so much easier to show the students afloat and then show pictures of those which you don't have in your area first

SOURCES FOR FURTHER INFORMATION: G20 G48 G13

ABOARD
☾ ☾
☾ ☾

ASHORE
☾ ☾

THEORY
☾ ☾

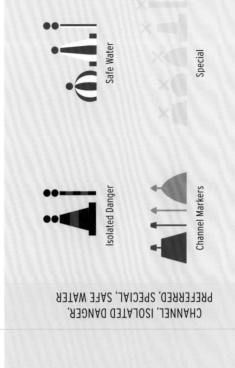

CHANNEL, ISOLATED DANGER, PREFERRED, SPECIAL, SAFE WATER

Isolated Danger

Safe Water

Channel Markers

Special

IALA CARDINALS

CARDINAL BUOYS

THEORY: TRAILING A BOAT:

AIM: Be able to prepare a boat on a trailer ready for trailing

LEVEL 1: KNOWLEDGE OF

LEVEL 2: UNDERSTANDS

· Approach into strongest element

· Communicate to crew their action on arrival and departure

LEVEL 1: UNDERSTANDS

LEVEL 2: CAN

· Use springs to bring stern off jetty

LEVEL 2: CAN

· Assess angle and speed of approach

· Make fast alongside

FUNDAMENTALS:

☻ Identify an escape route

☻ Prepare warps ready for arrival

☻ Brief crew and confirm understanding

ABOARD

ASHORE

THEORY

CONSIDERATIONS FOR LESSON PLANS:

· Maintain all round look out for other water users

· Shallow approach, minimum speed, prepare lines

· Check lines are secured in boat prior to securing ashore

DISPLACEMENT BOAT:

· Remember to use fenders if required

· May want to use a spring line to bring boat alongside

TILLER STEER:

· Same as RIB

Its easier to put way on, than to take way off. Approach slowly, use neutral as the favoured gear

SOURCES FOR FURTHER INFORMATION: G20 G48 G13 RYA WEBSITE

LAUNCH AND RECOVERY

KNOTS:

AIM: How to tie the basic knots of the scheme

LEVEL 2: CAN

· Bowline
· Fasten to a cleat
· Round turn and two half hitches
· Clove hitch

FUNDAMENTALS:

◐ Ensure all ends are whipped or heat sealed
◐ Ensure length of rope is long enough

ABOARD
◐ ◐ ◐

ASHORE
◐ ◐

THEORY
◐

CONSIDERATIONS FOR LESSON PLANS:

Have spare warps available for practice
· Adequate spare ropes for practise on and off the boat
Always
· Always practise your knots

SOURCES FOR FURTHER INFORMATION: G20 G48 G13 RYA BOOK OF KNOTS

KNOTS

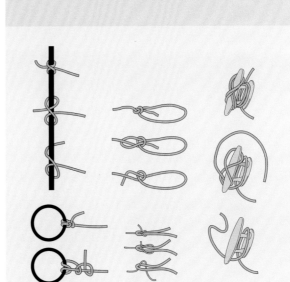

KNOTS

10 TOP TIPS FOR LEVEL 1 AND LEVEL 2 TUITION – RATIO 3:1

1. Ensure the kill-cord is worn correctly around the leg and is an appropriate length

2. Always sit in the "instructor position" where you have access to the kill cord and keep eye contact with the students when talking to them.

3. Never say DO NOT. Always focus on DO IT THIS WAY or DO IT THAT WAY show them what to do rather than what not to do!

4. Good demonstrations are effective but should be brief. Remember that you should use a demonstration with minimum talk in real time so they watch, then tell them what you did. Then they practice. Let them try but do not pounce on mistakes. By discussion try to get the students to identify what they did. ASK – DISCUSS - SOLVE.

5. Educate - one hand steer, one hand gear so best practices are instilled from the onset. When turning at low speed - steer then gear.

6. Always stress good communication in the boat, before starting off, powering up, powering down, turning or awareness of other water users.

7. Adopt the instructor position - sat by the kill cord wherever possible but definitely in a position where you can control the boat if things go astray.

8. Try to get the students to do everything with the instructor orchestrating the session. Only where manual dexterity is required, like tying a knot, should the instructor should get involved.

9. The instructor should use the boat as a training aid. Everything can and should be taught in the boat and then discussed later if consolidation is required.

10. Emphasise that it's easier to put way on, than to take way off, the favoured gear when slow speed handling is neutral.

LEVEL 2 DIRECT ASSESSMENT

The Powerboat Logbook G20 mentions that any candidate with the necessary experience may gain the Level 2 Certificate by direct assessment, rather than through a two day Level 2 course.

This approach is most likely to be seen when the certificate is needed as the basis of an International Certificate of Competence or when an experienced powerboat handler wishes to gain the higher awards in the National Powerboat Scheme.

The test may be undertaken at any RYA recognised Powerboat Teaching Establishment, using either a boat provided by the establishment or the candidate's own boat, subject to its approval by the assessor as suitable. Assessment will follow the format of the practical test shown below, and will be carried out by the principal or an RYA Powerboat Instructor nominated by him/her. In addition, candidates will be required to answer a theory paper to test their background knowledge. Before the test, the assessor should remind the candidate that the manoeuvre of coming alongside downwind/downtide is regarded as unseamanlike, but is tested because it may be necessary in an emergency.

CRITERIA FOR ASSESSMENT

The notes below provide the basis for assessing ability during the practical part of the test in terms of required and desirable performance. If a candidate fails to show any of the required performance criteria the assessor may not award a pass on that section of the test. Further attempts may be made. If a candidate fails to show any of the desirable criteria points listed, their attention should be drawn to them in their debrief. These criteria may also be used as guidance to the standard required during a full Level 2 Course.

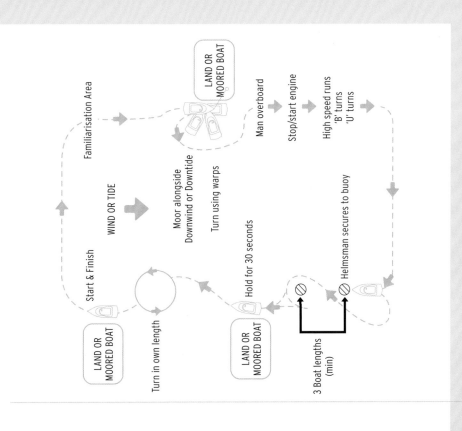

TASK	REQUIRED PERFORMANCE	DESIRABLE PERFORMANCE
FOR ALL TASKS	• Correct use of the kill-cord • Awareness of other water users • Complete the task • Consider aborting the manoeuvre early	• Effective communication with the crew
COMING ALONGSIDE	• Prepare warps/fenders or check crew have done so • Choose correct angle of approach • Control speed of approach • Stop boat in required place • Maintain control of boat while warps are secured	• Check security of warps
TURNING USING WARPS	• On hard sided boats prevent contact between boat and jetty/pontoon etc usually use reverse • On RIB's use warps to tie in front so the boat pivots. Can use forwards or reverse. Forwards puts less force on the crew • Secure boat adequately	• Position fenders effectively on hard sided boats Use sponsons on RIB's if safe to do so
MAN OVERBOARD RECOVERY	• Observe MOB or instruct crew to do so. Correct direction and speed of approach • Make suitable contact with MOB • Stop engine before attempting retrieval	• Execute immediate turn to keep prop away from MOB
STOP/START ENGINE	• Choose suitable area • Check gear/throttle/choke before starting • Start engine successfully • Check engine water cooling after starting • Warn crew before moving off	• Shift into neutral and check all around before stopping engine

TASK	REQUIRED PERFORMANCE	DESIRABLE PERFORMANCE
HIGH SPEED MANOEUVRES (IF APPROPRIATE)	• Choose suitable area • Warn crew before each manoeuvre • Look around before S and U turns • Control speed on U turns	• Initiate planing effectively • Trim boat properly • Deal with cavitation on turns
SECURING TO BUOY	• Choose correct angle of approach • Control speed of approach • Secure boat effectively • Depart from mooring safely	• Prepare warp
MANOEUVRING ASTERN	• Steer boat effectively in reverse • Control speed to avoid swamping over transom	• Move weight forwards to raise the stern if practicable
HOLDING OFF	• Maintain position to within 1/2 boat length • Pause in neutral during gearshifts • Avoid damage to engine or gears	• Start parallel to and approx 1 m off jetty/pontoon • Use gears calmly
TURNING IN OWN LENGTH	• Demonstrate understanding of principles • Pause during gearshifts	• Apply steering lock before engaging gear. Steer then gear
COMING ALONGSIDE – DOWNWIND/DOWNTIDE	• Preparation of warps/fenders • Choose correct angle of approach • Control speed of approach • Stop boat in required place • Maintain control of boat while warps were • Secured	

Note that the of coming alongside downwind/downtide manoeuvre is regarded as unseamanlike, but is tested because it may be necessary in an emergency.

SAFETY BOAT COURSE

The aim of this course is to introduce the techniques used in powerboats escorting racing fleets of dinghies, windsurfers and canoes, providing safety and rescue cover for training fleets and assisting in race management. It is strongly recommended that a member of the rescue crew should hold a first aid certificate (or should have experience of first aid) and a VHF operators licence.

As participants must hold the RYA National Powerboat Certificate Level 2, In some cases the course organiser may have to arrange for some or all participants to take the short Direct Assessment for the certificate before the Safety Boat course starts.

The emphasis throughout the course is on practical work, so that participants can experience and solve real problems, rather than simply discuss them. Practical sessions should be structured following the pattern of "Demonstrate - Practice - Test" outlined earlier, with the instructor posing real problems to the group involving the recovery of dinghies and windsurfers. The opportunity should be given for every participant to supervise each type of rescue outlined in the syllabus.

Ropework should be introduced as needed, rather than all being covered in one session. For example, the rolling hitch could be introduced in the briefing prior to a towing session, while heaving lines could be practised prior to the recovery of a dinghy on a lee shore.

Boats should be equipped appropriately for their operating area, using the list in the G44 Safety Boat Handbook as a guide. Dinghies and windsurfers must be available for practising rescue techniques.

SAFETY BOAT COURSE

FUNDAMENTAL CONCEPTS ONLY - SEE G44 - SAFETY BOAT HANDBOOK AND …

SPECIFIC RESCUES TECHNIQUES

INTRODUCTION TO THE BOAT:

AIM: To demonstrate the equipment which should be carried on safety boats to carry out their role as support/safety boats:

SAFETY BOAT: CAN

- The appropriate dress for safety crews
- Always have two crew on board
- Why the need for additional equipment
- What additional equipment
- Where to stow equipment

FUNDAMENTALS:

- Kill cord, correct length, works and spare carried
- Know how to use emergency equipment
- Use of bridle for towing
- Knowledge of knots for specific purposes

ABOARD

ASHORE

THEORY

CONSIDERATIONS FOR LESSON PLANS:

Additional equipment to be carried for safety boats

- Knife
- Extra warps
- Bridle
- Suitable anchor fitted
- Consider a portable bilge pump for emptying dinghy hulls
- Consider binoculars if covering large distances
- Throw line
- Tow line
- Flares

Always

- Check fuel levels – always use more fuel when towing
- Check first aid kit with survival bag
- Check expiry date of flares and fire extinguisher

SOURCES FOR FURTHER INFORMATION: G44 - SAFETY BOAT HANDBOOK

RYA FIRST AID MANUAL

SAFETY BOAT

SAFETY BOAT

Remember that the candidates attending this course are already qualified. Nevertheless, you are teaching new skills and should be in instructor mode for this course. Remember that this course requires a lot of different equipment plus suitably qualified people to use it whilst the module is being delivered

BOAT HANDLING – A VARIETY OF RESCUE SCENARIOS:

AIM: To simulate a number of rescue techniques for the candidates to practice:

SAFETY: CAN
- Drive the boat effectively
- Use the engine and elements to best effect to get boat into position
- Is aware of engine and pivot points when manoeuvring
- Always turns engine off when anyone in the water is in proximity to the boat

FUNDAMENTALS:
 Correct length and use of kill-cord
 Be aware of people in the water
 Pivot points and use of engine and elements
 One hand steer one hand gear
 Steer before gear
 Communication
 Dressed appropriate for conditions and prepared to enter the water if required
 Wear a buoyancy aid

ABOARD

ASHORE

THEORY

CONSIDERATIONS FOR LESSON PLANS:

Additional
- Use real sailors and windsurfers etc if possible rather than the candidates or yourself
- Show the candidates around the various equipment ashore prior to going on the water so they can familiarise themselves with the rigging etc
- Consider land drills prior to going afloat

Always
- Control the sessions
- Watch for fatigue and skill fade
- Ensure when someone is in the water near the boat the engine is off
- The crew wears buoyancy aids rather than life jackets
- The crew are dressed to enter the water
- Keep sessions short and focussed, the time will slip away if you are not careful

SOURCES FOR FURTHER INFORMATION: G13 G44

RESCUE SCENARIO

10 TOP TIPS FOR SAFETY BOAT TUITION – RATIO 6:1

1. Ensure the kill-cord is worn correctly and ready to be used when crews are in the water around the boat at all times

2. Familiarise the students with the equipment ashore prior to organising the rescue afloat.

3. Organise additional equipment and personalities for the course if you don't have the equipment or the skills yourself.

4. Ensure the safety boat crews are dressed to enter the water. A buoyancy aid is essential. Dry suits or alternative suitable clothing matched to the conditions are recommended.

5. Keep the sessions short and ensure everyone attempts each of the rescue scenarios.

6. Control - Do not allow crews to capsize without your knowledge and only then in a controlled environment you must control the various sessions afloat.

7. Never conduct a real man overboard procedure. Use a dummy or a substitute. If you are going to demonstrate how to retrieve a person from the water into the boat, the engine must be off and then the person enters the water and stays in contact with the boat.

8. When teaching total inversion in a dinghy, keep the safety crew and the safety boat away from the dinghy until the helm and crew from the dinghy are located.

9. When teaching on the water within the ratios 6:1, with two boats, control the other boat, a good briefing is essential, use of signals and on water communications is essential.

10. Always have at least two persons in the safety boat. The driver steers the boat the other effects the rescue. They should concentrate on their individual jobs. Use the crews of the other vessel to best effect.

INTERMEDIATE DAY NAVIGATION IN POWERBOATS

COURSE DURATION: TWO DAYS.

TAUGHT AT: ADVANCED POWERBOAT TRAINING CENTRES

TAUGHT BY: ADVANCED POWERBOAT INSTRUCTORS

ELIGIBILITY: Minimum age 16. Students should be able to demonstrate boat-handling skills to the level of the National Powerboat Certificate Level 2 Coastal. It is strongly recommended that candidates hold a first aid certificate and VHF operators certificate.

• This course is only to be taught at Advanced recognised training centres.

• This course is taught by Advanced Instructors. There is no "Intermediate Instructor" level.

• The vessel used must be equipped to the standards required to operate Advanced courses.

• It is recognised that each training centre's area of operation is different and therefore the chief powerboat instructor and principal should formulate operating procedures for this new course.

• There is no commercial endorsement applicable to this course.

The main teaching aim of this course is to equip the student with a sound understanding of daytime passage planning and they will be able to execute a passage plan created by them on the course.

As an Advanced Instructor you will be able to teach most of the subjects covered in this course. You should teach subjects in this course to a similar standard to that on the Advanced course. Your students may already have been through the Level 2 course and will be attending this course to further their own knowledge and skills, so rather than repeating Level 2 standard exercises introduce subjects at a higher level. Some guidance is given below.

Passage planning on this course should be a combination of traditional navigation including Course to Steer (CTS) and Electronic navigation methods.

KNOWLEDGE OF NAVIGATION
The following two subjects could be combined into one.

TRUE AND MAGNETIC BEARINGS
Explain how to apply both East and West variation, to a bearing read from the chart and to a bearing read from the compass. Get the students to do a few examples using different variation values.

BEARING AND DISTANCE
Using the Compass Rose on the chart and measurement of distance using the Latitude on the edge of the chart. Get the student to plot a course over ground from a given point to another given point and calculate the True bearing, Distance, and estimated time that it would take with a given speed. You may wish to extend this to magnetic bearing as well.

CHART SYMBOLS
Get your students to study the chart for your area of operation and identify five or more hazards to navigation. Then get them to identify five good points of interest that would assist them in making a safe passage. A copy of Admiralty Chart 5011 is a great aid in this exercise and should be available.

TIDAL DIAMONDS & TIDAL STREAMS
Give each of your students a Tidal Diamond on your local chart. Set the scenario such as follows; "It is now two hours after High Water you have broken down and are drifting. You know your position to be at Tidal Diamond #', calculate your position in one hours time. Does this present you in danger?'

SPECIFIC POINTS TO TEACH

• CAN use a plotting instrument to plot a course to steer (CTS). Breton or Portland style plotters are quite successful on fast planing craft.
• CAN implement IRPCS 5,7,8,9, 12-19, 23 Additional rule to Level 2 is Rule 23
• Rule 23 Power-driven vessel underway
• CAN use GPS waypoint navigation and determine
  – XTE – Cross Track Error
  – SOG – Speed Over Ground
  – COG – Course Over Ground
  – BTW – Bearing to Waypoint
  – DTW – Distance to Waypoint

Simple exercises should be created. Ideally, across tide to enhance the live correctional effect of the GPS compared to the traditional course to steer.
A comparative example could be:

1. Plot a course over ground to a clearly identified mark. On this leg do not take into account the tide. Steer the boat on the bearing derived from the chart and observe the sideways movement of the vessel, it is suggested that this exercise is carried out across the tide and at slow speed.

2. Plot traditional course to steer (CTS). Starting from the same point of origin repeat the exercise above.

3. Input the latitude and longitude position of the identified mark in exercise 1 as a waypoint in the GPS. Starting from our original position repeat the exercise this time using the GPS data for course correction.

• Explain how to make a VHF emergency call.

• If you are in any doubt refresh your memory and learn the mayday procedure off by heart. Remember as the instructor in charge of the boat you may be called upon to make the call one day.
• Knowledge of effects of waves. Explain how waves form and why they are worse in certain reaches than others. Talk about Head seas and Following seas. Trim down in head seas, Trim up in following seas.
• Knowledge of rougher conditions. Only put to sea in conditions that you know you are capable of teaching in. If you go out in rougher conditions make sure that you can deliver the required information. If it is too rough you will not only be putting you and your crew into unnecessary danger, and you may well put them off boating forever. Do not try to create rough conditions using the wash of another boat. Not only does this provide a false environment it also presents a serious risk of collision. If it is flat calm revert to a well-prepared theory lesson.
• Mooring stern-to, between posts and Med style.
• Many of your students will now keep their vessel afloat in marinas in the UK and increasingly abroad.

Most marinas welcome schools to practice mooring situations during quieter times but always remember to get permission first.

Med Style mooring is the practice of reversing towards your berth, usually a marina wall or pontoon; on your approach you deploy your anchor allowing the vessel to reach the wall. Attach your stern lines and then tension up your anchor to hold you a short distance away from the wall. Often marinas will have permanent mooring lines in place that you hook up with your boat hook whilst reversing into the berth. This is then attached to the bow instead of dropping the anchor.

• Remember as with all good passage planning, plan for the unexpected return in the dark. On this course you are not going to teach night navigation to the depth of the Advanced Certificate but you should prepare your students with basic light recognition and advice on getting back in the dark.

INTERMEDIATE DAY CRUISING COURSE

INTRODUCTION TO THE BOAT:

AIM: To demonstrate the equipment which should be carried on any boat to make it effective to carry out its role for day cruising over longer passages:

INTERMEDIATE: KNOWLEDGE OF
- Additional safety equipment to be carried
- Carrying flares as safety equipment

INTERMEDIATE: UNDERSTANDS
- Why the need for greater boat checks for failing light and longer passages
- How to make a mayday call
- Safely stow all equipment

INTERMEDIATE: CAN
- Additional equipment to be carried for longer passages
- Additional check of boat for failing light conditions

FUNDAMENTALS:

- Kill cord, correct length, works and spare carried
- Know how to use emergency equipment
- Charts are carried and waterproofed

ABOARD

ASHORE

THEORY

CONSIDERATIONS FOR LESSON PLANS:

Additional equipment to be carried for longer passages
- Adequate additional clothing
- Food and drink
- Charts and plotting instrument
- Money etc

Always
- Consider state of tide for return to slipway
- Essential to consider an "opt out" plan – bolt holes
- Get good, local weather report and plan accordingly
- Check fuel and or take spare or money to fill up
- Check marina facilities during route – fuel / water etc
- **Recommend to the candidates that they attend a VHF course**

SOURCES FOR FURTHER INFORMATION: G20 G48 G13

DISPLACEMENT BOAT

Remember that the candidates attending this course are already qualified. Let them do everything as far as possible. Interject if they are unsure or are attempting new skills. You should shift out of the "instructor" didactic manner into a coaching "mentoring", "facilitator" style. You should use questions as much as possible to try and get the students to build on their experiences

LAUNCHING AND RECOVERY:

AIM: Be able to launch and recover a boat off and on to a trailer safely and be aware of slipway dangers

INTERMEDIATE: KNOWLEDGE OF
· Launching and recovering in failing lights
· Condition of slipway

INTERMEDIATE: UNDERSTANDS
· Alternative methods of launching

INTERMEDIATE: CAN
· Launch and recover in a variety of conditions
· Communication at all times

FUNDAMENTALS:
 Choose correct method for slipway and boat
 Have a backup plan
 Assess, communicate, check understanding
 Ensure winch is serviceable on trailer

ABOARD

ASHORE

THEORY

CONSIDERATIONS FOR LESSON PLANS:

Additional thoughts regarding launch and recovery:
· Assess level of competence regarding the launch. Did they complete one on their level 2 course? If not you may have to teach this lesson using some of the group who have
· Adequate time to launch and recover
· State of tide on slip when due to recover
· Lighting of slipway in case or late return

Always
· Consider state of tide for return to slipway
· Essential to plan "opt out" plan – bolt holes
· Get good, local weather report and plan accordingly
· Check fuel and or take spare or money to fill up

SOURCES FOR FURTHER INFORMATION: G48 G13

LAUNCH FROM TRAILER
WITH TOW LINE

During this initial practical session you should start to build rapport with the students and assess their level of competence in a non testing environment. Talk to each candidate assess their experience and make a mental note of each one. These mental notes will be used on the water when their practical skills are demonstrated. Wet notes and pencil are especially useful now

BOAT HANDLING – EFFECTS OF WAVES:

AIM: Be able to drive a boat at safe speed in rougher conditions ensuring safety and comfort of crew and awareness of other water users:

INTERMEDIATE: UNDERSTANDS

- Use of power trim to use engine to best effect
- Trim UP in following sea
- Trim DOWN in a head sea
- Use of throttle up and down waves
- Loading of boat – balance and trim

INTERMEDIATE: CAN

- Drive boat safely
- Communicate with crew

FUNDAMENTALS:

☝ Control boat speed ensuring crew are safe and comfortable

☝ One hand steer one hand gear

☝ Communication and all round vision

☝ Trim the boat for sea state

ABOARD
☝ ☝ ☝

ASHORE
☝ ☝

THEORY
☝

CONSIDERATIONS FOR LESSON PLANS:

Additional information:

- The helm should consider wearing goggles in spray and rain
- Use the power trim to raise or lower the bow
- If the sea state is too rough re consider plan

Always consider the following:

- Re assess the plan
- Consider the sea state for recovery, would an alternative site be prudent or practicable
- When in doubt – don't go out
- Tide and wind direction – wind over tide conditions

SOURCES FOR FURTHER INFORMATION: G20 G13

These are new skills at intermediate level. You may need to teach the use of power trim as some may not have used this prior to this course. Some may have only used tiller steer. Some may not be used to a rib assess and teach accordingly

TRIM TABS RIGHT

TRIM TABS TOO FAR UP

BOAT HANDLING – MOORING ALONGSIDE MARINA BERTH:

AIM: Be able to moor alongside in a marina berth:

INTERMEDIATE: UNDERSTANDS

· Use of warps and springs to berth or depart in marina berth ahead or astern

INTERMEDIATE: CAN

· Assess wind and tide when approaching
· Brief crew and prepare lines
· Use warps to turn boat in marina berth

FUNDAMENTALS:

🕐 One hand steer, one hand gear
🕐 Brief the crew, consolidate understanding
🕐 Always protect the engine and propeller
🕐 Prepare all lines and have an opt out plan

ABOARD
🕐 🕐 🕐

ASHORE
🕐 🕐

THEORY
🕐

CONSIDERATIONS FOR LESSON PLANS:

Additional

· Ensure they assess angle of approach for coming into marina berth assessing wind and tide
· Make them aware of pivot points when turning close to other vessels – sponsons swinging

Always

· Consider abort plan early
· Consider driving past first before going in if unsure
· Use neutral as the favoured gear – Its easier to put way on than take way off
· Assess tide and wind and clearly brief crew on plan
· Look out for any other movement prior to slipping lines
· Ensure engine is running prior to slipping lines

SOURCES FOR FURTHER INFORMATION: G20 G13

These are new skills unless they did marina berthing on Level 2 or they completed their level 2 abroad – Ascertain if they have or have not completed this. This will effect your teaching plan of this section. They may have driven a different hull shape which behaves differently. Assess and coach. Use their experience

A. Approaching into wind will naturally slow the boat. The momentum of the boat will help it slide sideways alongside the berth.
B. Then turning momentum will tend to slow the boat away from the berth.
C. As the stern seeks reverses in astern, this boat professes easily into the birth.
D. The wind will push the craft into the berth, so care is needed not to overshoot. Put a stern line on early.

SEQUENCE

MOORING ALONGSIDE MARINA BERTH

BOAT HANDLING – MOORING STERN TO MED STYLE:

AIM: Be able to moor the boat Med style with the stern into the pontoon:

INTERMEDIATE: UNDERSTANDS
- Use of the anchor to hold the bow in Med style berth

INTERMEDIATE: CAN
- Drive the boat in reverse to moor stern to
- Assess wind and tide when approaching
- Brief crew and prepare lines

FUNDAMENTALS:
- Control the bow by use of the anchor Med style
- One hand steer, one hand gear
- Brief the crew, consolidate understanding
- Always protect the engine and propeller
- Prepare all lines and have an opt out plan

ABOARD

ASHORE

THEORY

CONSIDERATIONS FOR LESSON PLANS:

Additional
- Are there lines ashore which can be used for stern to berth
- Are there mooring buoys in the water instead of using anchor for stern to berth
- Ensure they assess angle of approach
- Make them aware of pivot points when turning close to other vessels
  - sponsons swinging

Always
- Consider abort plan early
- Practice anchoring first prior to attempting mooring stern to
- Consider driving past first before going in if unsure
- Use neutral as the favoured gear – Its easier to put way on than take way off
- Assess tide and wind and clearly brief crew on plan
- Look out for any other movement prior to slipping lines
- Ensure engine is running prior to slipping lines

SOURCES FOR FURTHER INFORMATION: G20 G13

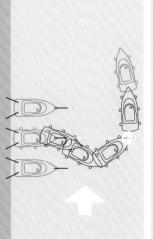

**MOORING STERN TO
MED STYLE**

These are new skills unless they did marina berthing on level 2 or they completed their level 2 abroad. Ascertain if they have or have not completed this. This will effect your teaching plan of this section. They may have driven a different hull shape which behaves differently. Assess and coach. Use their experience

MAN OVERBOARD:

AIM: Is able to return to the MOB using the correct approach, aware of miss procedure and getting person into boat

INTERMEDIATE: UNDERSTANDS

· An alternative method to recover MOB

INTERMEDIATE: CAN

· Recover MOB from the water in a variety of conditions

FUNDAMENTALS:

〇 As soon as contact is made turn engine off

〇 Turn into MOB to keep propeller away

〇 Crew keep watch on MOB at all times

ABOARD
〇 〇 〇

ASHORE
〇

THEORY
〇

CONSIDERATIONS FOR LESSON PLANS:

The basic technique is like picking up a mooring but without taking the tide into consideration

Additional:

· When MOB is alongside "turn engine off"

· Create enough room to make a controlled approach

· Consider approaching from upwind and let RIB drift onto MOB

· Teach one method which suits the RIB you are using and then explain the other technique – demonstrate if the boat is suitable then let the students practice

If you fall overboard inflate lifejacket and raise arm

SOURCES FOR FURTHER INFORMATION: G20 G48 G13

This is revision from Level 2 so there should be a level of competence. Ensure you do not over teach. Try to tease out the various techniques where possible from the students and put right any anomalies through general discussion rather than a formal "man overboard" lesson from the Level 2 syllabus. They should be competent at one method. Ensure they grasp an understanding of a different method and they do it practically

HI-LINE TRANSFER

ANCHORING:

AIM: Is able to deploy and recover the anchor and check for holding using transits

INTERMEDIATE: UNDERSTANDS
· The different anchor types
· The parts of the anchor

INTERMEDIATE: CAN
· Types of anchors and stowage
· Weighing anchor

FUNDAMENTALS:
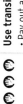 Approach against strongest element
 Prepare anchor and warp - chain or rope
Communicate with crew and select anchorage
Lower anchor and drift back or use reverse

ABOARD

ASHORE

THEORY

CONSIDERATIONS FOR LESSON PLANS:

Use transits or compass bearing to check holding
· Pay out a minimum of 5 times depth of water for rope
· Pay out a minimum of 3 times depth of water for chain

Is the tide on the flood or the ebb? If in doubt let out

SOURCES FOR FURTHER INFORMATION: G20 G48 G13

This is revision from Level 2 so there should be a level of competence. Ensure you do not over teach. Try and tease out the various techniques where possible from the students and put right any anomalies through general discussion rather than a formal "anchoring" lesson from the Level 2 syllabus

ANCHORING

08 THEORY:

AIM: To ensure the candidates can use GPS effectively

INTERMEDIATE: UNDERSTANDS
- Which publication contain the information they require, waypoints, tidal stream and heights, chart symbols, etc

INTERMEDIATE: CAN
- Use GPS navigation demonstrating XTE, COG, SOG, DTW, BTW

FUNDAMENTALS:
- Control
- Planning, tide, weather, back up plan
- Inform someone ashore

CONSIDERATIONS FOR LESSON PLANS:
Build in little scenarios - anchoring at an exact spot, fishing at an exact spot, entry into a port for lunch, entry into port and going alongside to buy lunch. If you make the trip as real as possible it will enjoyable and the students will see the reasons for the exercise.

ABOARD

Additional
- Ensure each candidate can enter waypoints into a GPS

ASHORE

Always
- Make the trip enjoyable
- Make sure they consider "Bolt hole" to "Safe havens" and program into GPS as a waypoint
- Pass the passage plan to someone ashore and give them an estimated finish time - and who to contact if not back
- Plan for return in failing light

THEORY

Always plan. Failing to plan is planning to fail
Have a back up plan
Leave a copy of all passage plans ashore with an estimated finish time and points of contact

SOURCES FOR FURTHER INFORMATION: G20 G48 G13
THE RYA NAVIGATION EXERCISES BY CHRIS SLADE AND SARA HOPKINSON

This is revision from Level 2 - nevertheless, taught to a higher level. They have to be competent with the use of GPS and be aware of its limitations. Although focus on the benefits of GPS

SOURCES OF WEATHER:

AIM: Can obtain a weather forecast from a variety of sources and knows how wind will effect the sea state

INTERMEDIATE: UNDERSTANDS
- How to interpret the shipping forecast
- The passage of a frontal system

INTERMEDIATE: CAN
- Where to get a detailed weather report
- Interpret the Beaufort wind scale

FUNDAMENTALS:
- Weather report for the whole area and the whole trip

This is in depth and additional competencies are required

ABOARD
€ €

ASHORE
€ €

THEORY
€ €

CONSIDERATIONS FOR LESSON PLANS:

Weather can change quickly. Be prepared
- Wind direction and tidal state will affect sea state
- Weather may effect recovery of RIB onto trailer
- Take additional clothing. It is always colder afloat
- Don't forget drinks and food for the trip

SOURCES FOR FURTHER INFORMATION: G20 G48 G13 RYA WEATHER HANDBOOK

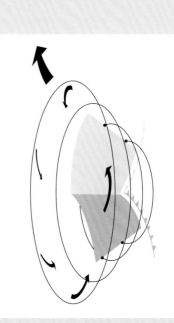

WEATHER

BOAT HANDLING – NAVIGATION BY A VARIETY OF MEANS:

AIM: To be able to use a variety of means to conduct a short coastal passage, plot position using electronic and traditional methods to ensure the helm knows where they are at any given time:

INTERMEDIATE: UNDERSTANDS

- Use of GPS to ascertain position

INTERMEDIATE: CAN

- Use GPS for XTE, COG, SOG, DTW, BTW
- Plot exact position by electronic and traditional means – GPS/chart plotter/compass
- Use timed runs, GPS, transits for navigation to a point
- Use GPS to
- Plot a course and make a pilotage plan
- Knows the importance of informing someone ashore of the plan and route

FUNDAMENTALS:

 Weather report and Tidal information

 Plan and check route

 Prepare pilotage plan

 Inform someone ashore and give an estimated return time

 Enter waypoints into GPS – Check Latitude and Longitude – (Should alleviate user error inputting waypoints)

ABOARD

ASHORE

THEORY

CONSIDERATIONS FOR LESSON PLANS:

If on day one you demonstrate to the candidates how to plan, plot and prepare, they have an example of what is expected. DO NOT set a navigation test to assess their level of skill.

Additional

- Ensure everyone drives and navigates
- Make the trip enjoyable. It is not a navigation test. It should be an enjoyable day trip in a RIB to get pleasure from being out on the water
- Consider anchoring for lunch in a specific spot. Use transits to fix that position and back up with GPS or chart plotter

Always

- When planning courses ensure the navigation exercise includes a cross tide route to demonstrate XTE and CTS for GPS and how to use transits to stay on course
- Use a variety of methods for navigation when afloat-timed runs, GPS, transits, etc
- Stop during a run and use traditional methods to fix position
- Stop during a run and use electronic method to fix position
- Always be aware of the tide and that when you slow the tide has more effect

The trip should be enjoyable and everyone should drive and navigate but don't ask them to do both at the same time. Encompass a variety of skills, anchoring, coming alongside, picking up a mooring, holding station which will enhance their boat handling skills but use them in a real life scenario.

SOURCES FOR FURTHER INFORMATION: G20 G48

THEORY:

AIM: To ensure the candidates are familiar with all the navigational techniques required to plan a short coastal passage by day and to make provision for a late return in failing light conditions:

INTERMEDIATE: UNDERSTANDS

· Which publications contain the information required, waypoints, tidal stream and heights, chart symbols, etc

· A variety of chart types, Admiralty and Imray

INTERMEDIATE: CAN

· Use traditional navigation plotting instruments to plan a short coastal passage

· Assess tidal heights and stream and the effects of wind

· Use GPS navigation demonstrating XTE, COG, SOG, DTW, BTW

· Use a plotter and determine true and magnetic bearings

· Calculate bearing and distance from the chart using dividers, plotter and compass rose

· Can use tidal diamonds from the chart

· Can use an admiralty tidal curve for a standard port

· Identify chart symbols using Chart 5011

FUNDAMENTALS:

 Control, planning, tide, weather, Plan "B"

 Inform someone ashore

ABOARD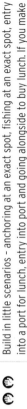

ASHORE

THEORY

CONSIDERATIONS FOR LESSON PLANS:

Build in little scenarios – anchoring at an exact spot, fishing at an exact spot, entry into a port for lunch, entry into port and going alongside to buy lunch. If you make the trip as real as possible it will be enjoyable and the students will see the reasons for the exercise.

Additional

· Make each candidate enter a port if possible

· Make each candidate plan a part of the route on their own

· Ensure each candidate can enter waypoints into a GPS

Always

· Make the trip enjoyable

· Make sure they consider "bolt hole" to "safe havens"

· Pass the passage plan to someone ashore and give them an estimated finish time – and who to contact if not back

· Plan for return in failing light

Always plan. Failing to plan is planning to fail. Remember this always. Have a back up plan and be prepared for circumstances that may require you to use it.

SOURCES FOR FURTHER INFORMATION: G20 G48 G13

THE RYA WEATHER HANDBOOK BY CHRIS TIBBS

THE RYA NAVIGATION HANDBOOK BY TIM BARTLETT

THE RYA NAVIGATION EXERCISES BY CHRIS SLADE AND SARA HOPKINSON

10 TOP TIPS FOR INTERMEDIATE COURSE TUITION – RATIO 6:1

1. Ensure the kill-cord works, is worn correctly around the leg and is of the correct length.

2. Remember that this is a teaching course. Always keep this in the back of your mind when teaching and when planning the course.

3. Set achievable aims for the sessions and create a learning environment.

4. Demonstrations should be kept to a minimum. Show in full time with some explanation, then talk through what you did. Then let them practice without interjecting. Then consolidate. ASK – DISCUSS - SOLVE

5. Pre plan the routes and demonstrate how you planned them. Then, let the students plan, create and drive the routes they have planned. Don't jump on mistakes – if it's safe to do so, let the students learn from their own mistakes.

6. Ensure that each of the candidates plan, drive and navigate at various times.

7. Always plan the course, have a back up plan and be adaptable.

8. Introduce a variety of navigational techniques – time speed distance, GPS, transits, pilotage. Show them the difficulties of navigation in an open sports boat.

9. Develop an understanding of recovery in failing light and discuss safety implications.

10. Ensure you have a safety plan in place.

ROUTE CARD TOP TIPS:

1. Keep the words to a minimum
2. Make it BIG Large print is best
3. Consider using diagrams
4. What do you need to know?

• From • To • Lat and Lon • Characteristic • Distance • Bearing

• Time • Hazards on route

ADVANCED POWERBOAT DAY AND NIGHT

COURSE DURATION: TWO DAYS INCLUDING ONE NIGHT PASSAGE

TAUGHT AT: ADVANCED POWERBOAT TRAINING CENTRES IN PLANING CRAFT

TAUGHT BY: ADVANCED POWERBOAT INSTRUCTORS

ELIGIBILITY: MINIMUM AGE 17.
- Students should be able to demonstrate boat handling skills to the level of the National Powerboat Certificate Level 2 Coastal with a thorough knowledge of navigation and chartwork to the level of Day Skipper Shorebased certificate.
- Candidates are required to hold a first aid certificate and VHF operator's certificate.

- This course is only to be taught at Advanced recognised training centres.
- This course is taught by Advanced Instructors.
- It is recognised that each training centre's area of operation is different and therefore the Chief Powerboat Instructor and Principal should formulate operating procedures to include the changes made to this course.

- **KNOWLEDGE OF** the differences for a twin-engine vessel.
If you are unfamiliar with twin-engine handling endeavour to broaden your knowledge both in practice and theory. Recommended reading on this subject is the Motor Cruising Practical Course Notes.

- **RESPONSIBILITY AS SKIPPER**
A requirement of the SOLAS V regulations is the responsibilities of the skipper for the organisation of the navigation, safety and welfare of the crew during the passage. As soon as a vessel leaves categorised waters SOLAS V requires that the skipper has prepared a passage plan. Although great detail is not required you should include the following;

- Are the crew fit to make the passage taking into account weather forecast, expected sea conditions and their experience?
- Do they have suitable clothing?
- Could the crew get the vessel to a safe haven without you?
- Do they know where all the safety kit is?
- Do they know how to use the VHF radio and make a mayday call?
- Do they have basic first aid skills?
- Have they been briefed in helicopter evacuation procedures?
- Is there enough food and water on board?

- **UNDERSTANDS** the use of chart plotters, radar, their advantages and limitations.
- It is recognised that most schools do not have Radar and it is not proposed that they should. However some students attend the advanced course to gain their commercial endorsement and many commercial craft will carry radar. As an advanced instructor you should endeavour to learn as much as possible about radar to be able to explain the basics. The RYA shorebased radar course is a good place to learn. Recommend to your candidates that they attend the radar course.
- Chart plotters are becoming common place on both commercial and small pleasure craft. They already form part of the Day Skipper shorebased course. Again learn as much as possible so that you can instruct with confidence. Two common questions asked are:
- What is the difference between Vector and Raster Charts?
- Can I see other boats on the screen?

- **CAN** use electronic navigation equipment for planning and undertaking a passage.
- This could include a similar exercise as in the Intermediate course.
- Plus introduce navigation along contours using the echo sounder. (An echo sounder is a requirement for the Advanced Course).

- **KNOWLEDGE OF** terms used in shipping forecasts, including the Beaufort scale, and their significance to small craft.
- Gain a full understanding yourself.
- Please teach as: "CAN" interpret a synoptic chart

- **UNDERSTANDS** sources of weather information and interpretation of forecasts including synoptic charts.
- Using the shipping forecast or inshore waters forecast for the day of the course, interpret the information relevant to your area of operation taking into account wind direction, direction of tide, is it springs or neaps?
- Using the synoptic chart for the day of the course teach your students what all the lines and symbols mean and how to use the synoptic chart to interpret the weather conditions.

- **CAN** apply the International Regulations for Preventing Collisions at Sea
- By the end of the course you must be satisfied that the student fully understands the rules of the road. Continuous testing throughout the course will establish the student's strengths and weaknesses. Concentrate on overcoming their weaknesses as a positive step to successful course completion. Remember that in order to fully assess the student's ability you must possess a complete understanding of the collision regulations.

- **KNOWLEDGE OF**
- How to change a propeller.
- Propeller pitch and diameter.
- Explain what pitch and diameter mean and how changing either dimension will affect the boat.
- Propeller ventilation and cavitation
- Explain the principles, causes and prevention of each.

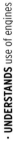

- **UNDERSTANDS** use of engines
- Many small craft are now fitted with diesel engines, especially those in commercial use.
- The course includes the operation of diesel engines. If you are unfamiliar with diesel engines the RYA Diesel Maintenance Course is a good place to start. The RYA publication on Diesel Engine Maintenance is a valuable resource in this subject.

- **UNDERSTANDS** Search Patterns.
- Following consultation with the MCA and RNLI the primary search pattern to be taught is the expanding box method. You may also wish to explain the sector search pattern. However, it is generally accepted that the expanding box method is an easier system to employ in a small fast craft.

- The RYA Training Chart Plotter used on Day Skipper Shorebased courses is available to advanced centres and will be a valuable classroom resource for this course.

- Other publications that are recommended to augment your student's knowledge of the subjects covered on this course are The RYA Weather Handbook by Chris Tibbs. The RYA Navigation Handbook by Tim Bartlett and RYA Navigation Exercises by Chris Slade and Sara Hopkinson.

ADVANCED POWERBOAT DAY AND NIGHT COURSE

INTRODUCTION TO THE BOAT:

AIM: To demonstrate the equipment which should be carried on any boat to make it effective to carry out its role for day cruising over longer passages:

ADVANCED: CAN

· Why the need for greater boat checks for failing light and longer passages
· Additional safety equipment to be carried
· Carrying flares as a source of safety equipment
· Additional equipment to be carried for longer passages
· Additional check of boat for failing light conditions

FUNDAMENTALS:

 Kill cord, correct length, works and spare carried

 Know how to use emergency equipment

 Charts are carried and waterproofed

 Spare batteries for torch / GPS etc

ALWAYS COMPLETED ON A PLANING BOAT:

ABOARD

CONSIDERATIONS FOR LESSON PLANS:

Additional equipment to be carried for longer passages

· Adequate additional clothing
· Food and drink
· Charts and plotting instrument
· Money etc

ASHORE

THEORY

Always

· Consider state of tide for return to slipway
· Essential to consider an "opt out" plan and "bolt holes"
· Get good, local weather report and plan accordingly
· Check fuel and or take spare or money to fill up
· Check marina facilities during route – fuel / water etc

SOURCES FOR FURTHER INFORMATION: G20 G13

Remember that the candidates attending this course are already qualified. Let them do everything as far as possible. Only interject if they are unsure or are attempting new skills. You should shift out of the "instructor" didactic manner into a coaching "mentoring", "facilitator" style. You should use questions as much as possible to try and get the students to build on their experiences

02 LAUNCHING AND RECOVERY:

AIM: Be able to launch and recover a boat off and on to a trailer safely and be aware of slipway dangers

ADVANCED: CAN

- Alternative methods of launching
- Launching and recovering in failing lights
- Condition of slipway
- Launch and recover in a variety of conditions
- Communication at all times

FUNDAMENTALS:

 Choose correct method for slipway and boat

 Have a backup plan

 Assess, communicate, check understanding

 Ensure winch is serviceable on trailer

ABOARD ⚫⚫⚫

ASHORE ⚫⚫

THEORY ⚫

CONSIDERATIONS FOR LESSON PLANS:

Additional thoughts regarding launch and recovery:

- Adequate time to launch and recover
- State of tide on slip when due to recover
- Lighting of slipway in case or late return

Always

- Consider state of tide for return to slipway
- Essential to plan "opt out" plan and "bolt holes"
- Get good, local weather report and plan accordingly
- Check fuel and or take spare or money to fill up

SOURCES FOR FURTHER INFORMATION: G20 G48 G13

LAUNCHING RIB

Building on existing skills. Nevertheless, introduce recovery at night or in failing light conditions

BOAT HANDLING – EFFECTS OF WAVES:

AIM: Be able to drive a boat at safe speed in rougher conditions ensuring safety and comfort of crew and awareness of other water users:

ADVANCED: CAN

- Use of power trim to use engine to best effect
- Trim UP in following sea
- Trim DOWN in a head sea
- Use of throttle up and down waves
- Loading of boat – balance and trim
- Drive boat safely
- Communicate with crew

FUNDAMENTALS:

- Control boat speed ensuring crew are safe and comfortable
- One hand steer, one hand gear
- Communication and all round vision
- Trim the boat for sea state

ABOARD

ASHORE

THEORY

CONSIDERATIONS FOR LESSON PLANS:

Additional information:

- The helm should consider wearing goggles in spray and rain
- Use the power trim to raise or lower the bow
- If the sea state is too rough re consider plan

Always consider the following:

- Re assess the plan
- Consider the sea state for recovery. Would an alternative site be prudent or practicable
- When in doubt – don't go out
- Tide and wind direction – wind over tide conditions

SOURCES FOR FURTHER INFORMATION: G20 G13

Building on existing skills. Nevertheless, rougher conditions should be introduced if possible

BOAT HANDLING – NAVIGATION BY A VARIETY OF MEANS:

AIM: To be able to use a variety of means to conduct a short coastal passage by day and night, plot position using electronic and traditional methods to ensure the helm knows where they are at any given time:

ADVANCED: CAN

- Use GPS to ascertain position
- Use GPS for XTE, COG, SOG, DTW, BTW
- Plot their exact position by electronic and traditional means – GPS/chart plotter/compass
- Use timed runs, GPS, transits, back bearings, soundings and clearing lines for navigation
- Use GPS for XTE, SOG, COG, DTW, BTW
- Plot a course and make a pilotage plan
- Knows the importance of informing someone ashore of the plan and route
- Use the echo sounder

FUNDAMENTALS:

☺ Weather report and tidal information

☺ Plan and check route and pilotage plan

☺ Inform someone ashore and give an estimated return time

☺ Enter waypoints into GPS - check Latitude and Longitude - (Should alleviate user error inputting waypoints)

ABOARD ☺ ☺ ☺

ASHORE ☺ ☺ ☺

THEORY ☺ ☺ ☺

CONSIDERATIONS FOR LESSON PLANS:

If on day one you demonstrate to the candidates how to plan, plot and prepare, they have an example of what is expected. DO NOT set a navigation test to assess their level of skill. Teach rather than assess.

Additional

- Ensure everyone drives and navigates
- Make the trip enjoyable. It is not a navigation test and should be an enjoyable trip in a RIB to enjoy being out on the water
- Consider anchoring for lunch in a specific spot. Use transits to fix that position and back up with GPS or chart plotter

Always

- When planning courses ensure the navigation exercise includes a cross tide route to demonstrate XTE and CTS for GPS and how to use transits to stay on course
- Use a variety of methods for navigation when afloat timed runs, GPS, transits, etc demonstrate as many methods as possible
- Stop during a run and use traditional methods to fix position
- Stop during a run and use electronic method to fix position
- Be aware of the tide - when you slow the tide has more effect

The trip should be enjoyable and everyone should drive and navigate. Don't ask them to do both at the same time. Cover a variety of skills, anchoring, coming alongside, picking up a mooring, holding station to enhance their boat handling skills.

SOURCES FOR FURTHER INFORMATION: G20 G13 GPS AFLOAT, RYA NAVIGATION EXERCISES

Building on existing skills and teaching lights and developing navigation techniques at night

BOAT HANDLING – SEARCH PATTERNS:

AIM: Be able to conduct a search using one method and have an understanding of others:

ADVANCED: UNDERSTANDS
- The sector search

ADVANCED: CAN
- Carry out the expanding box search

FUNDAMENTALS:
- Use of a chart datum
- Use of the compass
- Effect of tide
- Use of timings in expanding box

ABOARD

ASHORE

THEORY

CONSIDERATIONS FOR LESSON PLANS:

Additional
- You may lose the datum so use something expendable
- Set up a little exercise if you have time – make it realistic

Always
- Try and be realistic
- Don't set unachievable searches
- Keep it simple and short

SOURCES FOR FURTHER INFORMATION: G20 G13

Building on existing skills and teaching lights and developing navigation techniques at night

EXPANDING SEARCH PATTERN

Expanding Square Search
D=75% of expected casualty detection range

Labels on diagram: 3D, D, 2D, 4D, 3D, 3D

SOURCES OF WEATHER:

AIM: Can obtain a weather forecast , knows terms used in shipping forecast and knows how wind will effect the sea state

INTERMEDIATE: KNOWLEDGE OF
· Terms used in the shipping forecast
· Interpret the Beaufort wind scale

INTERMEDIATE: UNDERSTANDS
· How to interpret the shipping forecast including a synoptic chart
· The significance of barometric trend

FUNDAMENTALS:
€ Obtain a detailed weather report prior to planning the trip
€ Check the wind speed and tidal state - wind over tide situation

ABOARD
€

ASHORE
€ €

THEORY
€ €

CONSIDERATIONS FOR LESSON PLANS:

Weather can change quickly be prepared
· Wind direction and tidal state will affect sea state
· Weather may affect recovery of RIB onto trailer
· Take additional clothing. It is always colder afloat
· Don't forget drinks and food for the trip

SOURCES FOR FURTHER INFORMATION: G20 G48 G13 RYA WEATHER HANDBOOK

Developing existing knowledge

COOL AIR

WARM AIR

COLD AIR

Sunshine & showers   Heaviest rain ahead Cloud lowers and
of cold front. Drizzle   thickens

Barographic Trace

Barometer readings as fronts pass

SYNOPTIC CHART

THEORY:

AIM: To ensure the candidates are familiar with all the navigational techniques required to plan a short coastal passage by day and night:

ADVANCED: KNOWLEDGE OF
· Twin-engine vessel

ADVANCED: UNDERSTANDS
· Radar, shipping forecast, synoptic chart

ADVANCED: CAN
· Which publications contain the information required, waypoints, tidal stream and heights, chart symbols, etc
· A variety of chart types, Admiralty and Imray
· Use traditional navigation plotting instruments to plan a short coastal passage
· Assess tidal heights and stream and the effects of wind
· Use GPS navigation demonstrating XTE, COG, SOG, DTW, BTW
· Use a plotter and determine true and magnetic bearings
· Calculate bearing and distance from the chart using dividers and plotter and compass rose
· Can use tidal diamonds from the chart
· Can use an admiralty tidal curve for a standard port
· Identify chart symbols using Chart 5011

ABOARD

ASHORE

THEORY

CONSIDERATIONS FOR LESSON PLANS:

Build in little scenarios – anchoring at an exact spot, fishing at an exact spot, entry into a port for lunch, entry into port and going alongside to buy lunch. If you make the trip as real as possible it will be enjoyable and the students will see the reasons for the exercise.

Additional
· Make each candidate enter an unfamiliar port if possible
· Make each candidate plan a part a route on their own

Always
· Make the trip enjoyable
· Make sure they consider "bolt hole" to "safe havens" during daylight and night
· Pass the passage plan to someone ashore and give them an estimated finish time – and who to contact if not back
Always plan. Failing to plan is planning to fail. Remember this always. Have a backup plan.

SOURCES FOR FURTHER INFORMATION: G20 G13
THE RYA WEATHER HANDBOOK BY CHRIS TIBBS
THE RYA NAVIGATION HANDBOOK BY TIM BARTLETT
THE RYA NAVIGATION EXERCISES BY CHRIS SLADE AND SARA HOPKINSON
THE MOTOR CRUISING PRACTICAL COURSE NOTES
GPS AFLOAT

Building on existing skills and teaching lights and developing navigation techniques at night

THEORY:

AIM: Engine maintenance and propeller care:

ADVANCED: KNOWLEDGE OF
· Propeller pitch and diameter
· Cavitation and ventilation
· How to change a propeller

ADVANCED: UNDERSTANDS
· Use of different types of engines, outboard, Z drive, inboards, diesel, petrol, 2 strike, 4 stroke

ADVANCED: CAN
· Explain a variety of hull shapes and their advantages and disadvantages

FUNDAMENTALS:
 Use the propeller on the boat to explain pitch and diameter – a spare propeller is a useful addition
 Use real models if possible, look in the marina boat park and pick out the different drives and hull shapes

ABOARD

ASHORE

THEORY

CONSIDERATIONS FOR LESSON PLANS:

Additional
· Have access to a variety of propellers if possible
· Tour the marinas at every opportunity to discuss types of drives and hulls

Always
· Take the opportunity to ask questions and look at other craft and drives both on and off the water
· Try and build in a visit ashore to a marina where boats will be on the shore

SOURCES FOR FURTHER INFORMATION: G20

G25 - RYA DIESEL ENGINE MAINTENANCE HANDBOOK
Z003 - RYA OUTBOARD ENGINE BOOK

Building on existing skills and developing a knowledge of the propeller

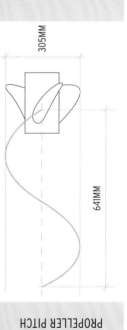

PROPELLER PITCH

305MM

641MM

10 TOP TIPS FOR ADVANCED COURSE TUITION – RATIO 6:1

1. Ensure the kill-cord works, is worn and is of the correct length

2. Keep all the candidates involved and maintain continual assessment

3. Remember, this is a teaching course and although students may have attended the shore based navigation course they could be used to planning at slow speed and you may need to fill any gaps

4. Set an imaginative and achievable navigational plan encompassing as many elements of the course as possible. Build on the Intermediate Day Cruising course

5. Consider discussing with each of the students where their particular weaknesses are and try and focus on those BUT ensure you cover the syllabus.

6. Try to plan two night runs if possible. Demonstrate how to plan and execute on the first evening and get them to plan and execute one on the second night.

7. Consider setting some pre-course work for the candidates – lights, shapes, navigation etc. You may want them to work out some tidal heights as well

8. Ensure you have all the equipment required for the course. Have a pre-conceived plan and consider a back up plan

9. You can use a non instructor in the other boat but they must be competent and have local knowledge of the area of operation

10. Make the trip enjoyable, set small scenarios en-route, anchor for lunch, visit unfamiliar ports by day and night and ensure someone ashore knows the route and escape routes. Consider a practical search and practice all navigational techniques.

05

INSTRUCTOR AWARDS AND LOGBOOK

INSTRUCTOR AWARDS
AND LOGBOOK

In the following pages you will find a useful guide to session planning. There is guidance on the content of each session and information on where to find additional material to enhance your teaching. There is a useful guide to help you decide where to deliver your subject either aboard, ashore or as theory. It is deliberately not prescriptive as it is recognised that each instructor will develop their own delivery style.

RECORD DETAILS OF YOUR CERTIFICATES HERE:

QUALIFICATION	VENUE	DATE
RYA POWERBOAT LEVEL 1		
RYA POWERBOAT LEVEL 2		
COASTAL ENDORSEMENT		
PLANING/DISPLACEMENT		
RYA SAFETY BOAT COURSE		
RYA INTERMEDIATE POWERBOAT COURSE		
RYA ADVANCED POWERBOAT COURSE		
RYA MEMBERSHIP NUMBER		
FIRST AID COURSE TYPE AND EXPIRY DATE		

NATIONAL POWERBOAT SCHEME INSTRUCTOR LOG

DATE	TYPE OF BOAT	HOURS INSTRUCTING	LEVEL OR COURSE	MAX WIND SPEED	CONFIRMATION (PRINCIPAL)
	TOTAL C/F		TOTAL B/F		

NATIONAL POWERBOAT SCHEME INSTRUCTOR LOG

DATE	TYPE OF BOAT	HOURS INSTRUCTING	LEVEL OR COURSE	MAX WIND SPEED	CONFIRMATION (PRINCIPAL)
	TOTAL C/F		TOTAL B/F		

NATIONAL POWERBOAT SCHEME INSTRUCTOR LOG

DATE	TYPE OF BOAT	HOURS INSTRUCTING	LEVEL OR COURSE	MAX WIND SPEED	CONFIRMATION (PRINCIPAL)
	TOTAL C/F		TOTAL B/F		

NATIONAL POWERBOAT SCHEME INSTRUCTOR LOG

DATE	TYPE OF BOAT	HOURS INSTRUCTING	LEVEL OR COURSE	MAX WIND SPEED	CONFIRMATION (PRINCIPAL)
TOTAL C/F			TOTAL B/F		

NATIONAL POWERBOAT SCHEME INSTRUCTOR LOG

DATE	TYPE OF BOAT	HOURS INSTRUCTING	LEVEL OR COURSE	MAX WIND SPEED	CONFIRMATION (PRINCIPAL)
	TOTAL C/F		TOTAL B/F		

NATIONAL POWERBOAT SCHEME INSTRUCTOR LOG

DATE	TYPE OF BOAT	HOURS INSTRUCTING	LEVEL OR COURSE	MAX WIND SPEED	CONFIRMATION (PRINCIPAL)
	TOTAL C/F		TOTAL B/F		

NATIONAL POWERBOAT SCHEME INSTRUCTOR LOG

DATE	TYPE OF BOAT	HOURS INSTRUCTING	LEVEL OR COURSE	MAX WIND SPEED	CONFIRMATION (PRINCIPAL)
	TOTAL C/F		TOTAL B/F		

APPENDIX 1 - CHILD PROTECTION

INTRODUCTION

RYA Recognised Training Centres are required to have a formal child protection policy which is checked as part of their annual inspection. Your organisation is therefore strongly advised to take the following steps:

Adopt a policy statement that defines the organisation's commitment to providing a safe environment for children.

Produce a simple code of practice and procedures governing how the organisation runs.

The RYA publishes guidelines to help clubs and training centres to enable children and vulnerable adults to enjoy the sports of sailing, windsurfing and power boating in all their forms, in a safe environment. They can be copied or adapted to meet the requirements of the organisation. The document can be downloaded from the RYA's website, www.rya.org.uk, under Working with Us.

The RYA Policy Statement on Child Protection is as follows:

As defined in the Children Act 1989, for the purposes of this policy anyone under the age of 18 should be considered as a child. The policy also applies to vulnerable adults.

It is the policy of the RYA to safeguard children and young people taking part in boating from physical, sexual or emotional harm. The RYA will take all reasonable steps to ensure that, through appropriate procedures and training, children participating in RYA activities do so in a safe environment. We recognise that the safety and welfare of the child is paramount and that all children, whatever their age, gender, disability, culture, ethnic origin, colour, religion or belief, social status or sexual identity, have a right to protection from abuse.

The RYA actively seeks to:

- Create a safe and welcoming environment, both on and off the water, where children can have fun and develop their skills and confidence.
- Support and encourage recognised training centres, affiliated clubs and class associations to implement similar policies.
- Recognise that safeguarding children is the responsibility of everyone, not just those who work with children.
- Ensure that RYA-organised training and events are run to the highest possible safety standards.
- Be prepared to review its ways of working to incorporate best practice.

We will:

- Treat all children with respect and celebrate their achievements.
- Carefully recruit and select all employees, contractors and volunteers.
- Respond swiftly and appropriately to all complaints and concerns about poor practice or suspected or actual child abuse.

This policy relates to all employees, contractors and volunteers who work with children or vulnerable adults in the course of their RYA duties. It will be kept under periodic review. All relevant concerns, allegations, complaints and their outcome should be notified to the RYA Child Protection Co-ordinator.

NOTE FOR PRINCIPALS – GOOD RECRUITMENT PRACTICE

If a good recruitment policy is adopted, and the issue of child protection covered in the organisation's risk assessment, both children and adults should be adequately protected. Potential abusers have difficulty operating in a well-run organisation.

All applications, whether for paid or voluntary work, should be subject to an appropriate level of scrutiny. The RYA's view is that the level of checking you carry out should be proportionate to the role and the level of risk involved. The risk may be higher if the person will be in regular contact with the same child or children, in sole charge of children with no parents or other adults present, and/or in a role involving authority and trust, such as an instructor or coach.

The organisation should agree a clear policy on:
• who to check
• the level of check to be conducted for each category
   – references
   – self-disclosure
   – Enhanced Criminal Records Disclosure
and then apply it fairly and consistently.

CRIMINAL RECORDS CHECKS

If you are appointing someone to a high risk role, you can ask the prospective employee or volunteer to apply for a Criminal Records Disclosure. This can also be undertaken for existing staff or volunteers. Organisations affiliated to or recognised by the RYA can access the Disclosure process through the RYA. The procedure varies according to the home country and legal jurisidication in which your organisation is located (for example in Scotland criminal records checks are mandatory in some circumstances). Full up to date information is available from the RYA website, or contact the RYA's Child Protection Co-ordinator.

RESPONSIBILITIES OF STAFF AND VOLUNTEERS

Staff or volunteers should be given clear roles and responsibilities. They should be aware of your organisation's child protection policy and procedures and be given guidelines on:

- following good practice (see RYA Guidelines for Good Practice Guide)
- recognising signs of abuse.

INDENTIFYING CHILD ABUSE

The following brief notes provide a guide to help you identify signs of possible abuse and know what action to take in such cases. The RYA Child Protection Guidelines on the RYA website cover the subject more fully.

Forms of abuse

Child abuse is a term used to describe ways in which children are harmed, usually by adults and often by people they know and trust. It refers to damage done to a child's physical or mental health. Child abuse can take many forms:

__Physical abuse__ where adults or other children physically hurt or injure children (eg. by hitting, shaking, squeezing, biting or burning), give children alcohol, inappropriate drugs or poison, or attempt to suffocate or drown children.

__Neglect__ includes situations in which adults fail to meet a child's basic physical needs (eg. for food, water, warm clothing, essential medication), consistently leave children alone and unsupervised, or neglect children emotionally by failing or refusing to give them love, affection or attention.

__Sexual abuse__. Boys and girls are sexually abused when adults (of the same or opposite sex) or other young people use them to meet their own sexual needs. This could include: full sexual intercourse, masturbation, oral sex, fondling, showing children pornographic books, photographs or videos, or taking pictures for pornographic purposes.

Emotional abuse can occur in a number of ways, for example where there is persistent lack of love or affection, there is constant overprotection which prevents children from socialising, or children are frequently shouted at, criticised, taunted, bullied or pressured to perform at a level that the child cannot realistically be expected to achieve.

Bullying may be seen as deliberately hurtful behaviour, usually repeated or sustained over a period of time, where it is difficult for those being bullied to defend themselves. The bully may often be another young person. Although anyone can be the target of bullying, victims are typically shy, sensitive and perhaps anxious or insecure. Sometimes they are singled out for physical reasons - being overweight, physically small, having a disability or belonging to a different race, faith or culture.

RECOGNISING SIGNS OF POSSIBLE ABUSE

It is not always easy, even for the most experienced carers, to spot when a child has been abused. However, some of the more typical symptoms which should trigger your suspicions would include:

- unexplained or suspicious injuries such as bruising, cuts or burns, particularly if situated on a part of the body not normally prone to such injuries
- sexually explicit language or actions
- a sudden change in behaviour (eg. becoming very quiet, withdrawn or displaying sudden outbursts of temper)
- the child describes what appears to be an abusive act involving him/her
- a change observed over a long period of time (eg. the child losing weight or becoming increasingly dirty or unkempt)
- a general distrust and avoidance of adults, especially those with whom a close relationship would be expected
- an unexpected reaction to normal physical contact

• difficulty in making friends or abnormal restrictions on socialising with others.

It is important to note that a child could be displaying some or all of these signs, or behaving in a way which is worrying, without this necessarily meaning that the child is being abused. Similarly, there may not be any signs, but you may just feel that something is wrong.

LISTENING TO THE CHILD

Children may confide in adults they trust, in a place where they feel at ease.

Always:

• stay calm – ensure that the child is safe and feels safe
• show and tell the child that you are taking what he/she says seriously
• reassure that child and stress that he/she is not to blame
• be careful about physical contact, it may not be what the child wants
• be honest, explain that you will have to tell someone else to help stop the alleged abuse
• make a record of what the child has said as soon as possible after the event
• follow your organisation's child protection procedures.

Never:

• rush into actions that may be inappropriate
• make promises you cannot keep (eg. you won't tell anyone)
• ask more questions than are necessary for you to be sure that you need to act
• take sole responsibility – consult someone else (ideally the designated Child Protection/Welfare Officer or the person in charge or someone you can trust) so that you can begin to protect the child and gain support for yourself.

What to do if you are concerned about a child or about the behaviour of a member of staff

A complaint, concern or allegation may come from a number of sources: a child, their parents, someone else within your organisation. It may involve the behaviour of one of your volunteers or employees, or something that has happened to the child outside the sport, perhaps at home or at school. An allegation may range from mild verbal bullying to physical or sexual abuse. If you are concerned about what is happening to a child, there are simple flow diagrams in the RYA Guidelines which take you through the actions you should take.

If you have noticed a change in the child's behaviour, first talk to the parents or carers. It may be that something has happened, such as a bereavement, which has caused the child to be unhappy. However if there are concerns about sexual abuse or violence in the home, talking to the parents or carers might put the child at greater risk. If you are concerned that a child may be being abused, it is NOT your responsibility to investigate further, BUT it is your responsibility to act on your concerns and report them to the organisation's Child Protection/Welfare Officer or person in charge, who will make the decision to contact Children's Social Care (formerly Social Services) or the Police and report to the RYA Child Protection Co-ordinator.

If you are concerned about the behaviour of a member of staff or volunteer, inform the organisation's designated Child Protection/ Welfare Officer or the person in charge, who should follow the RYA's procedures. It may be necessary for the member of staff to be temporarily suspended while an investigation takes place.

It is important to understand that a member of staff reporting suspicions of child abuse, particularly by a colleague, may undergo a very high degree of stress, including feelings of guilt for having reported the matter. It is therefore very important to ensure that appropriate counselling and support is available for staff.

APPENDIX 2 - APPEALS PROCEDURE

All RYA qualified Instructors and Trainers are required to treat students and candidates with respect and fairness.

All assessments in the use of boats and their equipment have implications for the safety of participants. It is therefore essential that candidates be given a thorough and searching assessment. It would be dangerous to the candidate and anyone whom they subsequently teach if a Trainer erred on the side of leniency in awarding a certificate, There must never be any question of relaxing the standards required for an award.

REALISTIC AIMS

In some cases, it becomes clear to the Trainer at an early stage in the assessment process that the candidate has been over-ambitious in their choice of award. In such instances the Trainer should discuss the situation with the candidate and agree revised achievable aims.

GROUNDS FOR APPEAL

A candidate has grounds for appeal if he or she believes that:

- They have not been given a reasonable opportunity to demonstrate their competence ... or
- The person carrying out the assessment has placed them under undue or unfair pressure ... or
- That the Trainer has reached the wrong conclusion on the basis of the outcome of the candidates' performance in the assessment.

THE PROCEDURE

The candidate should first raise the concern with the Trainer to see if the matter can be amicably resolved. If it is inappropriate to consult the Trainer or if there is no amicable solution, the candidate should appeal in writing to the RYA Chief Powerboat Trainer within 20 working days of the assessment. The letter of appeal should contain the following:

- Full details of the assessment - when, where, involving whom etc
- The nature of the appeal
- Any supporting documentation relating to the assessment - outcome, action plans, reports etc.

On receipt of an appeal, an investigative process will commence. Following investigation, the candidate will be informed of the outcome, which will be one of the following:

- The original decision confirmed
- The assessment carried out again by the same or a different Trainer
- The original decision overturned and the assessment judged to be adequate

If the candidate is still unhappy about the decision, they may appeal against the outcome to the RYA Training Divisional Committee.

APPENDIX 3 – RESOURCES AND REFERENCES:

You may find the following publications useful for further reading, some of the texts from this book makes reference to a number of those listed below – All the books can be purchased through the RYA.

TITLE	AUTHOR	RYA REF
The Adlard Coles Book of Outboard Motors	Tim Bartlett Adlard Coles	ZO03
First Aid Manual (8th Edition Revised)	St Johns Supplies	ZF03
GPS Afloat	Bill Anderson Wiley	ZG05
RYA Book of Knots	Peter Owen Adlard Coles	ZK05
The RYA Book of International Certificate of Competence 2nd Edition	Bill Anderson Adlard Coles	ZI03
Reed's Nautical Almanac	Adlard Coles	ZM22
Skippers Handbook (Sail or Power) – Forth Edition	Malcolm Pearson Adlard Coles	ZS02
Seaman's Guide to The Rules of the Road	Morgan Technical Books	ZS09
RYA Yachtmaster© Shorebased Notes	RYA Training	YSN
RYA Day Skipper Shorebased Notes	RYA Training	DSN
RYA Inland Waterways Handbook	RYA Training	IWPCN
RYA Personal Watercraft Practical Course Notes	RYA Training	PWPCN
RYA European Waterways Regulations	Tam Murrell RYA Training	G17
RYA Practice Charts (N. Hemisphere)	RYA Training	Tba
RYA Training Almanac (N. Hemisphere)	RYA Training	TAN
RYA Boat Safety Handbook	RYA Training	C8
RYA Powerboat Handbook	Paul Glatzel	G13

RYA Safety boat Handbook	RYA Training	G16
RYA Powerboat Instructors Handbook	RYA Training	G19
RYA Powerboating Logbook	RYA Training	G20
RYA International Regulations for Preventing Collisions at Sea	RYA Training	G2
RYA VHF Handbook	RYA Training	G31
RYA Motor Cruising Handbook	Simon Jinks RYA Training	G24
RYA Introduction to Radar	RYA Training	G34
RYA Diesel Engine Handbook	Andrew Simpson	G25
RYA Navigation Handbook	Tim Bartlett	G6
RYA Weather Handbook	Chris Tibbs	G1
RYA Start Powerboating	Jon Mendez	G48
RYA Navigation Exercises	Chris Slade Sara Hopkinson	G7
RYA Manual of Seamanship	Tom Cunliffe RYA Training	G36
Symbols and Abbreviations used on Admiralty Charts	Admiralty	5011

APPENDIX 4 - RYA EQUALITY POLICY

OBJECTIVES

- To make boating an activity that is genuinely open to anyone who wishes to take part.
- To provide the framework for everyone to enjoy the sport, in whatever capacity and to whatever level the individual desires.
- To ensure that the RYA's services, including training schemes, are accessible to all, including those who have been under-represented in the past.

POLICY STATEMENT

The Royal Yachting Association is committed to the principle of equality of opportunity and aims to ensure that all present and potential participants, members, instructors, coaches, competitors, officials, volunteers and employees are treated fairly and on an equal basis, irrespective of their gender, age, disability, ethnic origin, colour, religion or belief, social status or sexual orientation.

IMPLEMENTATION

- The RYA encourages its affiliated clubs and organisations and its recognised training centres to adopt a similar policy, so that they are seen as friendly, welcoming and open to all.
- Appointments to voluntary or paid positions with the RYA will be made solely on the basis of an individual's knowledge, skills and experience and the competences required for the role.
- The RYA's full equal opportunities policy can be viewed at www.rya.org.uk

Approved by RYA Council 7 December 2005

APPENDIX 5 - POWERBOATING AND THE ENVIRONMENT

Boating in all its forms, not just under power, has the potential to impact on the marine environment. There is both national and international legislation that exists to ensure that the marine environment is protected and substantial penalties apply for breach of these laws. As instructors you are well placed to ensure new participants are aware of this and able to ensure we continue to enjoy freedom on the water.

Comprehensive information on both the legal and practical aspects, including products available, can be found at **www.rya. org.uk/knowledgebase/environment** and The Green Blue website at **www.thegreenblue.org.uk**. Here are a just a few tips that you can incorporate into your training.

REFUELLING AND DISCHARGING YOUR BILGE WATER

Discharge of oil or oily wastes into the water is an offence. Oils can enter the water during every day operations such as refuelling and pumping the bilge. Spill kits suitable for small craft are available and can easily be carried on board. As routine practice it is good to have oil absorbent 'socks' in the bilge to mop up any oil that finds its way there. Safety fill nozzles are also available for refuelling from portable tanks. If you do spill oil or fuel into the water, never use detergents this only adds to the pollutants in the water.

WASTE ON BOARD

Dumping waste at sea, even food waste within 3 miles of shore, is an offence. Ideally leave any excess packaging ashore before you leave for the day but secure all rubbish on board and ensure nothing blows over the side. If it does, practice your man over board skills! Use recycling facilities ashore where available, have a couple of separate bags on board to store your waste.

CLEANING

Washing down the boat at the end of the day can often be achieved by a little extra elbow grease. If detergents are used, choose more environmentally sensitive ones and avoid those that contain chlorine, phosphates or bleach. This also applies to detergents used in sinks and toilets on board. Take care to wash off trailers and hulls particularly when transporting boats as species can hitch-hike and cause major problems when they colonise a new area.

SPEED, WASH AND DISTURBANCE

Coastal and inland waterways play host to rich wildlife, many habitats and species are protected by law. Boat users enjoy freedom on the water, however, with freedom comes responsibility. If you come across wildlife whilst afloat, take care not to harass or damage it. Disturbance can affect feeding and breeding regimes. Think about your speed and the wash created when you are close to the shore to avoid erosion of habitats and disturbing feeding and nesting sites. Use recognised landing places when you go ashore

TOILETS ON BOARD

International laws regulate the use of sea toilets. Use shore based facilities wherever possible and never use sea toilets in marinas, rivers and low tidal flushing

RYA Membership

Promoting and Protecting Boating
www.rya.org.uk

RYA Membership

Promoting and Protecting Boating

The RYA is the national organisation which represents the interests of everyone who goes boating for pleasure.

The greater the membership, the louder our voice when it comes to protecting members' interests.

Apply for membership today, and support the RYA, to help the RYA support you.

Benefits of Membership

- Access to expert advice on all aspects of boating from legal wrangles to training matters
- Special members' discounts on a range of products and services including boat insurance, books, videos and class certificates
- Free issue of certificates of competence, increasingly asked for by everyone from overseas governments to holiday companies, insurance underwriters to boat hirers

- Access to the wide range of RYA publications, including the quarterly magazine
- Third Party insurance for windsurfing members
- Free Internet access with RYA-Online
- Special discounts on AA membership
- Regular offers in RYA Magazine
- ...and much more

Join now - membership form opposite

Join online at *www.rya.org.uk*
Visit our website for information, advice, members' services and webshop

1 Important To help us comply with Data Protection legislation, please tick *either* Box A or Box B (you must tick Box A to ensure you receive the full benefits of RYA membership). The RYA will not pass your data to third parties.

☐ **A.** I wish to join the RYA and receive future information on member services, benefits (as listed in RYA Magazine and website) and offers.

☐ **B.** I wish to join the RYA but do not wish to receive future information on member services, benefits (as listed in RYA Magazine and website) and offers.

When completed, please send this form to: RYA, RYA House, Ensign Way, Hamble, Southampton, SO31 4YA

2

Title	Forename	Surname	Date of Birth	Male	Female
1.			D D / M M / Y Y	☐	☐
2.			D D / M M / Y Y	☐	☐
3.			D D / M M / Y Y	☐	☐
4.			D D / M M / Y Y	☐	☐

Address

Town | **County** | **Post Code**

Evening Telephone | **Daytime Telephone**

email

Signature: _____ **Date:** _____

3 Type of membership required: *(Tick Box)*

☐ **Junior Membership** £13 (no reduction for direct debit)

☐ **Personal Membership** £39 or £36 by direct debit

☐ **Family Membership** £58 or £55 by direct debit

Family Membership: 2 adults plus any under 21s all living at the same address

4 Please tick ONE box to show your main boating interest.

☐ Yacht Racing   ☐ Yacht Cruising
☐ Dinghy Racing   ☐ Dinghy Cruising
☐ Personal Watercraft   ☐ Inland Waterways
☐ Powerboat Racing   ☐ Windsurfing
☐ Motor Boating   ☐ Sportsboats and RIBs

Please see Direct Debit form overleaf

Instructions to your Bank or Building Society to pay by Direct Debit

Please complete this form and return it to:
Royal Yachting Association, RYA House, Ensign Way, Hamble, Southampton, Hampshire SO31 4YA

To The Manager: _____ Bank/Building Society

Address: _____

_____

Post Code: _____

Originators Identification Number

9	5	5	2	1	3

5. RYA Membership Number (For office use only)

2. Name(s) of account holder(s)

_____

_____

3. Branch Sort Code

		—			—		

4. Bank or Building Society account number

Banks and Building Societies may not accept Direct Debit instructions for some types of account

6. Instruction to pay your Bank or Building Society
Please pay Royal Yachting Association Direct Debits from the account detailed in this instruction subject to the safeguards assured by The Direct Debit Guarantee.
I understand that this instruction may remain with the Royal Yachting Association and, if so, details will be passed electronically to my Bank/Building Society.

Signature(s) _____

Date _____

Cash, Cheque, Postal Order enclosed
Made payable to the Royal Yachting Association

£ _____

Office use only: Membership Number Allocated

077

Office use / Centre Stamp